Bar Stool Fiction:

20th Century Life in Little Egypt

Bar Stool Fiction:
20th Century Life in Little Egypt

by

Alvin Roberts

1stBooks - rev. 1/24/01

TABLE OF CONTENTS

PART ONE: STORIES FROM MY BAR STOOL

PART TWO: STORIES FROM MY NEIGHBOR'S BAR STOOL

CATHY, THE LIGHT OF MY LIFE

Author's note: The following dedicatory chapter was originally prepared for inclusion in *Coping With Blindness*, published by SIU Press in 1998. In a real sense, Cathy has inspired all of my works of fiction, at first through her physical presence and then through her memory.

•••••••••••••••••••••••••••••••

I began falling in love with Catherine Mary Dutke when I first heard her beautiful voice answer my phone call to the Visually Handicapped Managers of Illinois Office in 1982 and continued to love her more every day until her tragic, untimely death on August 9, 1995. This book would never be complete without, at least, a tribute to Cathy who, unconditionally, gave me unbounded love, psychological support, and total life commitment during the eight-and-one-half years of our marriage. Her love and devotion gave me the will to combat the creeping physical and emotional restrictions of advancing age, which enabled me to reciprocate her love and continue to make positive contributions to society such as the writing of this book. If I can convey even a vague impression of the momentous challenges Cathy overcame to accomplish the many life goals she set for herself, this brief sketch of her short life will be as inspirational and enlightening as any of the fictionalized accounts of the challenges encountered by workers with the blind and their clients characterized in *Coping With Blindness*.

One of the first things I remember Cathy's Father, Herman, saying to me during our first family visit was, "You have married a stout-hearted, loving girl." Over the years, I have deepened my understanding of Herman's description of his first-borne child. Her strong family values, willingness to take chances and strive mightily to achieve her goals, and total commitment to giving and receiving love were Cathy's life response to a loving nurturing family and neighborhood environment, basic religious teaching, and her unconquerable motivation to overcome the personal challenges and physical barriers created by her disability.

Herman Dutke, whose parents had arrived in North Dakota from Poland around the turn of the twentieth century, married Winifred Schultz, whose mother was one of five sisters who each homesteaded 1 quarter section of North Dakota prairie, on January 18, 1949. Both the Dutkes and Schultzs were devoted Catholics who integrated religious teaching into child rearing along with good manners and a strong work ethic. Therefore, the beautiful baby with pretty blond curls born to Herman and Winni on November 7, 1949 found herself in a family system conducive to healthy physical, psychological and spiritual growth. Little Cathy took to this fertile family soil like a duck to water, walking at twelve months and demonstrating her ability to recite nursery rhymes at her second family Thanksgiving dinner, which greatly pleased her maternal Grandfather, Frank Schulz, who also had a fabulous memory that enabled him to continue working as a cattle grader in Montana stock yards well into his eighties. She also learned conversational Ukranian from her Baba (the Ukranian word she learned for Grandma) who lived in a tiny house next door to Herman and Winnie. Baba played many Ukranian games with the bright, perky little girl, and I wonder if this early, pleasurable activity was the motivation for Cathy's spending so much time fascinating our grandchildren with creative games, ranging from blowing giant bubbles with six-year-old Sarah in the back yard to playing complicated board and word games with eleven-year-old Jessica and Sherry. Besides walking at twelve months and reciting nursery rhymes at two years, Cathy developed rapidly in other physical and social skills. She acquired a quick wit which she cultivated throughout her life, constantly amusing her friends and loved ones with thought provoking, tart responses to our trite and ambiguous statements.

Cathy entered the first grade in the Southhart school when Herman, a railway telegrapher, took his young family (now augmented by four-year-old, Frank, and two-year-old, Bernadette) into the living quarters of the Southhart Depot where he had accepted a position as station agent. Cathy had many fond memories of life in this depot: watching her father rapidly tap out messages on his telegraph key, running out to passing trains with typed train orders attached to a long pole which the conductor retrieved as the caboose rolled past, and being bathed in a warm tub of water, after which she was tucked into a warm bed.

Things went well until a cold, damp day in early March when Herman glanced up from his desk and saw Cathy running home from school, shivering from the cold. Rushing out and wrapping her in his coat, he took the little girl into the depot and gave her a warm drink. When Winnie, who had spent the day helping Baba (who still lived in Bellfield) cut out material for a dress, returned to prepare dinner, she noticed that Cathy had a fever. By the next morning, the fever had diminished, being replaced with a rash which Winnie recognized as measles. When the fever unexpectedly returned, Winnie consulted her handy child-rearing guide by Dr. Spock and immediately took her daughter to the Dickinson Hospital, where a new pediatrician from New York diagnosed encephalitis.

Cathy remained in a coma until Mother's Day. Because of the mounting hospitals bills, the child was released to be cared for at home until a supply of typhoid serum, which was being used to stimulate Cathy's immune system to cope with the encephalitis, could be procured. Winnie said she was working around the house, keeping the comatose child in her line of vision, when she was startled to hear Cathy say, "I wove you, Mamma." Cathy thought she had just been sleeping through the night, but she had actually been unconscious from March 2 until Mother's Day, forty days. Those four words, "I wove you, Mamma", were the most wonderful Mother's Day present Winifred Schultz-Dutke ever received. Due to the long period of inactivity, Cathy received physical therapy to restore muscle strength and coordination so she could resume walking and other physical activities. When it was noticed that she could pick up coins and other very small objects dropped on the floor but would bump into furniture, an ophthalmological examination revealed that Cathy had almost no vision in her left eye and a limited visual field in her right eye. By the time I became acquainted with her, this right visual field was limited to five degrees, which is similar to seeing the world through the center of a roll of paper towels. On the hundreds of walks we took during our eight happy years, Cathy always had me on her left arm so my cane could keep us from bumping into objects. Also, because she could not see obstacles very near her feet, she developed a stooped posture, which those who did not understand her visual condition attributed to an orthopedic impairment, but she actually leaned forward in order to see where she was stepping.

Although restoration of walking and other physical functions was necessary for Cathy to resume normal life activities, she demonstrated no reduction in memory and other mental capacities, reentering public school after completing first grade at home with instruction by a visiting teacher. She made good grades and generally adjusted well to life in Dickinson, North Dakota, becoming active in the Camp Fire Girls and the Candy Stripers (a teen-age hospital volunteer organization). Cathy spoke with pride of the valuable social lessons she learned from her family, particularly a consideration for others and an obligation to assume responsibility for her own decisions and actions. She had great admiration for the cooperative child supervision system practiced by the mothers of her neighborhood. According to Cathy, any Mom who caught a child misbehaving had full authority to correct the situation, and all the kids knew it. These mothers also cooperated in guaranteeing the safety and welfare of the neighborhood child pack. Besides the training in courtesy, thrift and responsibility taught at home and school, Cathy, Frank and Bernie learned early about special rules followed when visiting Grandmother Florence Schultz, educated as a teacher back in New York: "You must try at least one spoon full of each course at Grandmother's dinners. You must use good table manners and speak correctly." She never forgot many of these precepts. Cathy was the most considerate person I ever knew, and her knowledge and use of the English language were superb.

With all this social training influencing her character development, one might conclude that she would become a conservative conformist, unwilling to take chances or consider novel or unpopular ideas, but this was not the case. Consideration for the feelings and views of others and adherence to fundamental ethical and moral standards governed her social relationships, but these character traits in no way kept Cathy from striving to achieve the goals she set for herself, particularly her desire to build a life in which her identity was based on accomplishing and enjoying those things she would have pursued if she had not been disabled, no matter what risks or sacrifices were required. This compulsion to live unencumbered by her blindness is best illustrated by her life-long insistence on using the mode of transportation which most closely paralleled the automobile, without which most U.S. citizens could not transport themselves to their jobs or perform most other economic and social activities. Cathy demonstrated her determination to transport herself on a bicycle at an early age.

Although her younger brother, Frank, was roaming the neighborhood on a bicycle at age eight, Cathy was forbidden this mode of transportation because her parents understood her visual loss and feared she would injure herself. One day, Cathy quietly took Frank's bicycle to the top of the hill on Second Avenue West, mounted this two-wheel chariot and came to a screeching stop in front of the Dutke home at the corner of Second Avenue West and Ninth Street just as Winnie came down the front steps. This and subsequent demonstrations of her ability to manage a fast moving vehicle, although frightening to her parents, finally won Cathy permission to have her own bike. She continued to enjoy the freedom of bicycle travel throughout her life. Her last ride was to the Carbondale Memorial Hospital on August 7, 1995 for a routine blood test just a few hours before she experienced a ruptured brain aneurism which took her life.

Catherine Dutke graduated from Dickinson High School in 1968 and proceeded to complete the four-year teacher training curriculum at Dickinson State University in three years. Cathy's desire to become a teacher was based on her admiration for a succession of role models, including her Grandmother, Florence, and her Aunt, Anna, who also served many years as a county superintendent of schools in Eastern Montana. All during our marriage, she kept a hand-held school bell passed down through the Manning family (her grandmother's maiden name) to the next descendent who began teaching school. This bell has now been returned to Winifred so it can continue to symbolize the family commitment and support to the next descendent who carries it into a twenty-first century class room.

Teaching jobs were few and far between in North Dakota when Cathy entered the job market in 1971, but, with her true grit, she expanded her job search and landed a position in a one-room country school near Culberton, Montana. Winnie drove her adventurous young educator and her trunks filled with books and other belongings to the lonely outpost of frontier education known as the Mona School and left her after helping clean the teacher quarters and unpack. Cathy spent the school year without any means of transportation other than rides to shop in Culberton or Sidney provided by the parents of her eight students. At night and on week ends, she was totally alone and isolated, except when a class mate, Jonetta Wolfe, who taught several miles away and had a car, came to visit and compare notes on teaching materials and techniques. Cathy looked forward to these visits with her friend, who often drove her into town for dinner and a movie. Cathy said this experience of teaching grades one through eight taught her to improvise and organize her work effectively, which was immensely helpful during her future jobs where these skills made it possible to compete successfully with persons who had normal vision. The fact that she had to provide her own janitorial service and keep the furnace and other equipment functioning probably accounted for Cathy's ability to take the lead in many of our home repair and improvement projects after our marriage. Once, during a blizzard when no parents could reach the school house, it became necessary for Cathy to entertain the students for a couple of days while preparing food for them in her kitchen and making sure that the furnace kept burning and the pipes did not freeze. Often, when she related such dramatic incidents, I would suggest that she write an autobiography to inspire other visually impaired persons, but Cathy always seemed too busy living her life to take time out for writing a book.

Cathy interrupted her teaching career to spend 18 months in Orlando Florida, where she worked as a governess, after which she moved to St. Paul, Minnesota where she continued caring for children until she secured a teaching position in Strasberg, North Dakota, the home town of Lawrence Welk. She recalls Lawrence visiting the local drug store and talking with his friends as though he were still their neighbor instead of a visiting celebrity. Cathy's last teaching position was in the elementary school in Garison, North Dakota, where she taught for two years.

When Cathy and her sister, Bernie, who was then employed as a computer programmer by the Rail Road Retirement Board in Chicago, met at the Dutke home for Brother Frank's wedding to Patricia Mori, Bernie invited Cathy to return to Chicago for a visit. This visit changed the course of Cathy's career. She was fond of telling her acquaintances that she felt like a bird released from a cage when she discovered the Chicago transit system. For the first time in her life, she could travel independently to any work site or social engagement. Cathy immediately decided that she would never again live where accessible public transportation was not available (no more months of isolation in a lonely one-room school for her). She kept this pledge to herself until she gave up this freedom of mobility to marry and move to Carbondale, Illinois, where the only city transportation was an often unreliable taxi. Cathy constantly advocated for a public transportation system during her eight-and-one half years in Carbondale. It is very sad that a public bus system began operation the week of her death before she was able to take even one bus ride.

The Chicago transit system opened up a variety of job opportunities at wages far above Cathy's earnings as an elementary teacher of isolated rural schools. She once had a temporary position as a proctor for civil service examinations, which required her to travel three hours a day on a succession of elevated trains and buses. She was employed as an office manager for a child-care agency which dispatched retired women, many of whom had a wealth of child rearing experience because they were grandmothers, to provide temporary care for children of celebrities and other wealthy people on Chicago's Gold Coast. As we sipped coffee and watched the David Brinkly Sunday news commentary from our living room TV in Carbondale, she would often reminisce about baby sitting for George Wills, a regular Brinkly panelist.

About 1982, Catherine began experiencing a further reduction in the visual field of her right eye and decided to enroll in the clerical training program at the Chicago Light House for the Blind, where she could learn adaptive techniques which would enable her to continue working even if her vision continued to fail. It was during her Light House training that she met Donna Millard, who became her apartment mate and closest friend. They began spending a week end each December making mountains of cookies which they distributed to their families for Christmas. This marathon cookie bake became institutionalized after Cathy moved to Carbondale, incorporating the Roberts grandchildren and Donna's teen-aged nieces as baker apprentices.

About the time she completed the Light House clerical training, Sharon Howarton, her Vocational Rehabilitation Counselor, told Cathy of an opening with the Visually Handicapped Managers of Illinois, a corporation of blind managers of snack bars, cafeterias, and vending machine operations in both government and private facilities. Bob O'Shaughnessy, then director of training and personnel for this corporation, says Cathy was always striving to learn more and do her job better. She took a special interest in issues affecting the welfare of the blind managers and went beyond the call of duty in helping resolve these issues. Cathy demonstrated these same work characteristics along with a strong sense of loyalty and the ability to create harmony and understanding within the work force when she moved to the Illinois Visually Handicapped Institute in June of 1985. She served as my secretary and personnel liaison for this rehabilitation center for the adult blind until we were married and moved to Southern Illinois in April of 1987.

I am not sure when I first thought of asking for Cathy's hand in marriage. As superintendent of the IVHI, it was my job to prepare the annual budget, and Cathy and I spent many evenings working on this and other rush projects for our central office in Springfield. One evening, following a late budget session, when we were having dinner in a loop restaurant, we were chatting about how we wanted to spend the rest of our lives. I suddenly asked Cathy if she had ever thought about getting married, and, if she had, would she consider marrying me. To my delight and surprise, she said she thought being married to me might be the way she wanted to spend the remainder of her life.

We were married at the Bismark Hotel in Chicago on December 20, 1986, and the next eight-and-a-half years were the happiest period of my life. Cathy made my house into a home, she accepted my daughters and their children as hers, she helped me write and edit two books, completed a masters degree in Rehabilitation Counseling, and found time to give me understanding and love beyond my wildest expectation: all of this while working full time.

Cathy provided me with the most complete and satisfying relationship I have ever experienced with another human being by totally meeting my needs for a wife, lover and friend and making it possible through intimate communication for me to meet her needs. No arrangement of words on a page can convey the depth and completeness of our relationship to those who read this book, but they will immediately recognize it if they are ever lucky enough to engage the right mate, and they probably won't be able to describe it either.

CATHY'S TREE

Would that I could, I would be beside thee under Cathy's Tree,
There to somehow experience the comfort of thy presence bound
with the soothing perceptions of nature--
Not the sting of sleet,
Not the chilling dampness of cold rain,
Not the deep bite of winter wind--
But the feathery softness of snowflakes against our skin,
The caress of warm spring rain,
The bonding warmth of the summer breeze
And all other perceptions of nature which comfort
And soothe the soul and bind mates together.
Would that I could exist, body free, and still know thee,
We would dwell under Cathy's Tree for eternity.

To Cathy, The Light of My Life

INTRODUCTION

Readers of my other short story collections will recall that the settings for these narrations are usually social gathering places such as taverns. This is a well tested technique used as far back as *Canterbury Tales* and continued by more recent writers such as Washington Irving. The settings for these narrations are bars in Carbondale, Illinois, such as P.K.'s (short for Pizza King).

Because the tales in part One are based on events in which I was personally involved, and P.K.'s is located in a building in which a significant portion of my early life was spent, a few notes about the structure at 308 South Illinois Avenue may enhance the association of these yarns with their time and place in the twentieth century. This building was built in the 1930's to house a medical clinic. When the consortium of doctors practicing at this facility moved to the new hospital on West Main Street, the Illinois Department of Public Welfare rented it. I, along with an array of child welfare and other human service workers, were headquartered at this address until the mid-nineteen-sixties, when we moved to new quarters at 1200 West Main Street. About 1968, Gwyn Hunt and her husband Tom converted the building into a pizza parlor. Although the name of Pizza King (P. K.'s) has been retained, food service has been primarily supplanted by bar service coupled with breakfast and lunch service.

The rationale for the subtitle is the setting of these stories in the Southern Tip of Illinois, commonly referred to as Little Egypt. The area acquired this name as a result of a drought in Central Illinois in the early 1830s, which forced these farmers to haul seed corn from the Southern counties. This strategy for acquiring seed corn reminded many of the farmers of the Biblical account in Genesis of when the Israelites had to make a similar journey to Egypt for grain. An enterprising reporter published an account of the farmers' journey to Southern Illinois in the local paper and referred to the area as Little Egypt, a name which is still current for this region.

Living in the mid-twentieth century, the characters in these stories were influenced by prevailing institutions, such as religious fundamentalism, and local historical events. The connection between institutional teaching and historical events is illustrated by such cultural legacies as the connection between the journey to replenish seed grain in the 1830's and the Biblical story of the Israelites making a similar journey down into Egypt. Other events which have influenced the life styles of people residing between the Ohio and Mississippi rivers are the military victories of George Rogers Clark over the British Red Coats at Kaskaskia and Vincennes during the American revolution, and the strong current of support for the Confederacy during the Civil War, which left a tendency toward frontier rugged individualism and rebelliousness in our character. Perhaps the three-way conflicts among boot-leggers, the Ku Klux Klan and the justice system during Prohibition in the 1920's also contributed just a tinge of lawlessness in our collective character. The reader may recognize some of these character traits manifested in such actions as Charlie's attempt to preserve the symbolic value of the American Flag, the free-thinking approach to life attributed to Buck Brewer in "Plantin' Old Buck", and the Huckleberry Finn type fantacies acted out by the pre-adolescent characters in "Cool Under Pressure" and "Ride'em Cowboys".

The six tales in Part One are semi-autobiographical and adhere more closely to the facts because of my first hand involvement. In many instances, biographical material not directly connected to a particular story has been included to enhance narrative flow and plausibility instead of filling in these gaps with my imagination, which was the technique more commonly employed in Part Two because of my lack of personal involvement. For example, the description of the Victory Garden movement in World War II and my Mother's unfavorable reaction to my cousin's and my childish glee over the possibility of becoming war heroes when we heard of the bombing of Pearl Harbor were included in "Ride'em Cowboy" to provide a feeling for the impact of the war on the average American family and illustrate the way we kids tended to incorporate real life into our fantasies.

The selections in Part Two are based on interesting occurrences related by friends at social gatherings. These tales tend to rely more on imagination, current events at the time of the story and known geographical locations to create back ground and plausibility than those in part one, but they do tend to reflect the humor, habits, and pursuits of many people in the area of Illinois fondly known as Little Egypt. Some readers may question my decision to include "Plantin' Old Buck" in Part Two because they will have remembered from stories in Part One, such as, "Stashing the Cash", that Buck was my step-father. My reasoning was that I was not aware of this story until it was related to me at least twenty-five years after Buck's death by Charlie Downen. The ideas for "Daredevil" and "The Hungry Heard" were related to me by Kevin Cawthon and Gayle Johnson respectively. Vickie Hamman really came through in a pinch. When I told her that I just needed one more story plot to complete this collection, she immediately told the story outline for "Boatman's Lady." She also provided the plot for "Orchids For Vickie". Thank you all for supporting my writing habit.

Alvin Roberts
December 12, 1999

PART ONE
Stories from my Bar Stool

THE GREAT FIGHT PARTY

One morning in the spring of 1999, I received an unusual phone call from a colleague in the Office of Rehabilitation at the state capitol. When the secretary said Stan Johnson, who conducts in-service training programs, was on the line, I expected an inquiry about a staff training problem. Instead of asking about late training requests or some other deficiency, Stan said he was involved in a study of the early experiences and memories of elderly persons and felt I would be a most appropriate subject since I was completing my forty-fifth year in state employment.

After joking about Stan classifying me as an old geezer, I recounted several events from childhood. In the 1930's, there was only one radio station in Southern Illinois. The major portion of this station's (call letters, WEBQ) programming was live until the middle 1940's, and I recalled traveling about twenty miles in a Model A Ford to perform on a weekly barn dance program which featured aspiring country music stars from surrounding farms. Another social phenomenon which interested Stan was the interest and excitement exhibited by the public in air planes during the 1930's. If an air craft motor was detected by someone working in the garden or doing some other outside task such as pushing a manual lawn mower, that person would rush from house to house calling the occupants outside to see the flying machine. On at least one occasion a two-seated plane landed in a field just east of town, and the pilot spent the day taking those who were brave enough to be coaxed into the spare seat for a brief flight over the town for a price of two dollars.

Medicine shows were another form of entertainment during my childhood. An ancient truck with a covered bed would pull into a vacant lot, and the driver, with the help of his assistant (usually an attractive young woman), would arrange a portable stage on the rear of the vehicle, after which, they would go about town tacking up posters inviting the locals to a demonstration of the curative powers of a tonic with an exotic name. That evening the "Doctor," who had discovered a miraculous substance during his travels in some distant land, would explain how his miracle tonic had cured illnesses ranging from arthritis to deafness. Often, he would even produce letters of testimony from persons in neighboring towns who had experienced miracle cures. Sometimes, the pretty assistant would emotionally describe how the "Doctor" had discovered her languishing in a modern hospital near death from a fatal disease and had restored her to health and beauty with his life-giving tonic. As she recounted her story, the "Doctor" would pass through the crowd selling the tonic, which contained a generous portion of alcohol, for 50 cents a bottle. When the show was repeated on succeeding nights, it was not uncommon to witness testimonies from respected citizens, such as deacons of the church and business leaders, extolling the effects of the tonic which made them forget their aches and pains, become care free, and sleep "like a log".

Another strata of my ancient memory which Stan wanted to probe was the first radio programs I could remember. I recalled several soap operas, such as "Is There Life After Thirty Five?" This program told of a woman in her late thirties who was still able to find fame and romance, even though she had passed the prime of life. These programs appealed to the women in our neighborhood while my friends and I were more interested in adventure serials such as, "Jack Armstrong, The All American Boy," and "The Lone Ranger."

Stan's phone call seemed to open up a compartment in my memory containing snippets of radio shows I had not thought about for many years. Not that I remember actually hearing "The War of the Worlds," but I do recall my father and mother discussing it the next day. My dad was saying that he could not believe some people had actually believed the Martians were invading because the announcer stated that the program was simply a dramatization of the book by H. G. Wells.

2

Throughout the spring and summer of 1999, I have continued to be reminded of these early memories. Listening to a song, watching a TV show, or encountering a person or situation at work will trigger a childhood memory, such as hearing the broadcast of the prize fight between Max Schmelling and Joe Louis. The incident which evoked this memory was a TV documentary about the rise of Adolf Hitler. I recalled hearing a news cast from Germany in which a man was shouting in a strange tongue and the crowd was responding with something that sounded to me like "see Kyle," a kid who lived just across the alley and, as far as I knew, had never been seen by a German.

When I asked my uncle Thomas, who was employed by the government to teach the local farm boys how to make safe use of the electricity made available through the Rural Electrification Act, about this strange broadcast, he explained that the crowd had really been shouting, "Seig Heil." He said these strange words had nothing to do with my friend Kyle. They meant something like, "Conquer all," or "The Conqueror." He went on to tell me about a man named Hitler, the ruler of Germany, who thought his people were stronger than any other people on the earth. In fact, he said there would soon be a boxing match to settle the question as to whether the United States or Germany had the toughest men. The way Thomas explained it, this guy, Hitler, was going around bragging that his people were stronger, smarter and better looking than any other people in the world, and our hero, Joe Louis, had challenged Hitler's strong man, Max Schmelling, to a fifteen round fight to prove Hitler was full of hot air. This was not a sure thing, though; Schmelling had actually beaten Joe two years before, in 1936, when I was only six years old, which is probably why I didn't remember this earth shaking event.

Feelings ran high as the big night approached. The news papers had contained many articles by previous heavy weights analyzing the strategies Louis would need to defeat the German, who was chosen by Hitler to prove the invincibility of the Master

Race. When Schmelling had defeated Louis in 1936, Hitler invited him to dinner and bragged that his victory over Joe Louis proved that Arians were superior to all other people. It took the German heavy weight thirteen rounds to wear down The Brown Bomber, as Louis was known, so we were prepared for a long slug match when we gathered around the Philco AM radio perched on a high shelf in the living room of my uncle Paul Baxter's house on that warm June evening in 1938. Aunt Margie had popped a large mixing bowl of corn, Grandma set out a tray of cookies, and Mom contributed pitchers of ice cold lemonade. Dad tried to raise the excitement level by arranging some friendly wagers on the outcome of the fight, but it was very difficult to find anyone willing to bet on Schmelling because of the fierce loyalty to The Brown Bomber, who symbolized American patriotism. The radio signal was static free, but the volume fluctuated, almost becoming inaudible every few minutes. Expecting a long fight, uncle Paul said the fading out of the announcers voice would not keep us from hearing most of the action because the loud periods seemed longer than the silent intervals.

At last, the ring-side announcer introduced the fighters and said, "Shake hands, and come out fighting!" As soon as the opening bell sounded, the ring announcer began to shout that Joe was throwing one punch after another into the head and body of Schmelling. As the round continued, Max began to avoid some of Joe's punishing left hooks and jabs and even began to connect with a few of his own. It was at this point that the voice of the announcer faded out, and there was a long silence punctuated only by the frustrated swearing of the men in the room. The next audible words from the announcer were almost drowned out by the crowd noise, but it sounded like, "Joe Louis has knocked out Max Schmelling in 2 minutes and four seconds. Ladies and gentlemen, the new heavy-weight champion of the world, Joe Louis!" The announcer explained that Schmelling was being carried from the ring due to an apparent back injury from a hard body punch which connected above the kidney when Max suddenly turned his back to the champ to grasp the ropes for support.

In considering the Louis Schmelling broadcast from the perspective of the nineteen-nineties, with our big screen, high definition television sets, it is difficult to appreciate the enthusiasm engendered in that little group gathered around an AM radio which did not even transmit the most exciting moment of the fight. But when we remember that radio broadcasting was only about fifteen years old and networks were in their infancy, my father's evaluation of the heavy-weight fight broadcast of June 6, 1938 is not surprising: "We never heard the actual knockout, but it was sure better than waiting to read about it in the paper."

Alvin Roberts

COOL UNDER PRESSURE

"Mind if I ask you a personal question?" asked a quiet voice from the neighboring bar stool. I was ready for another conversationalist since Jill, the girl on my right with whom I had been discussing the process of writing procedural manuals for corporations, had gone home to feed her dog. Assuming the question was the one most frequently asked by strangers, "What is it like to be blind?", I suggested we introduce ourselves and order a drink before we began sharing personal information. My neighbor said her name was Dee and she was a psychology major, and her question was, how often did I encounter some one who really seemed to understand and accept blind people? This was a much more insightful question than I had anticipated. Before I could answer, she wanted to know how I obtained a personalized beer mug with the name of the bar, Pk's, and my name on it. Explaining that Gwyn Hunt, the bar owner, ordered these personalized mugs for regular customers at a cost of $15, I said Nate Silkwood, my son-in-law, had bought the mug with my name and BBS (which stands for Bureau of Blind Services, where I am employed). Further enlightening Dee on the virtue of these mugs, which hold 4 ounces more than the regular PK mugs, I ordered two fresh beers and proceeded to answer Dee's original question with a question.

"Have you ever had a best friend?" I asked. When she answered, "Several during different phases of my life," I asked what circumstances had created these "best friendships." Dee said that her best friends were people with whom she had shared very meaningful experiences and with whom she shared mutual trust based on intimate knowledge of each other's competencies, weaknesses and aspirations. "Were any of your best friends blind?" I asked.

"There weren't any blind kids around for me to form close relationships with," she replied. "How do you get to know blind people anyway?"

"You've answered your own question," I told her. "There are only about two blind persons per every 1,000 in the general population; so, you see, there just aren't enough of them to form accepting, understanding relationships with the other 998 sighted people per thousand, even if they wanted to have a blind, best friend."

Dee seemed to ponder my answer for several seconds. Then she said, "So, if there are so few blind people that most of us who see have no opportunity to know them, how do blind children ever learn to integrate with the sighted majority?"

"Some of us are lucky enough to develop a give-and-take relationship with a relative or friend which jump-starts us down the path of positive relationships with members of the sighted majority. But I can best illustrate this integration process by telling you a true story about my cousin, Jim Baxter." Dee asked me to hold the story until she could signal the bar tender for a refill. When our mugs were full, I told about one of the times Jim and I almost became accident statistics.

"Every blind boy should have a cousin like Jim," I told her. Jim was two years younger than me and a head shorter until he was about thirteen. Never living more than a block apart, we had played and fought together since before he could walk. I don't think he became aware of my blindness until he was three or four years old, when he began warning me about steps and other hazards on which he had seen me injure myself. He seemed to equate my blindness with some of his deficiencies, such as not being quite as tall or strong as I was, and began to collaborate with me in using his sight and other faculties to compliment my strength and size in accomplishing such tasks as building a wood fort, climbing trees, reaching through the neighbor's fence to swipe apples from his prize tree, and winning fights with other neighborhood kids. Once, when we were engaged in a rapid-fire rock fight with some young gentleman from the right side of the railroad tracks, I was standing just behind Jim to hand him rocks, and he accidentally put a permanent dint in my head as his arm came back for a long throw. But that is another story.

A catastrophe occurred one summer when we were learning to swim. Perhaps because Crab Orchard Lake was just five miles east of Carbondale, the city fathers had neglected to build a swimming pool, reasoning that any kid who wanted to swim would walk five miles to-and-from the lake. After all, healthy young boys often walked ten miles behind a plow and still had energy to walk the neighbor girls to church that evening. Jim and I had devised a strategy of camping out to minimize the walking in order to have more time and energy for swimming and other exciting activities such as picking fruit from the orchards of unsuspecting farmers and taking short cruises in row boats moored around the lake by fisherman. They would detach their out-board motors and leave their boats tied to a dock or tree at the water's edge. In order to leave plenty of time to pursue what ever interesting opportunities for adventure we encountered, Jim and I packed some bacon, potatoes, salt and pepper, coffee, a pot and skillet in two bed rolls consisting of two well-worn quilts, which we shouldered about ten A.M. and marched out of town toward Crab Orchard Lake. Our journey took us past Club Thirteen, a night club and gas station named after State Route 13, where we spent a nickel on a coke which we shared with two straws. We hitched a ride on the rear of a horse drawn wagon and arrived at the lake around noon. After helping ourselves to several ripe peaches from a road-side orchard, we made camp in some trees about a half mile south of a bridge which carried Route 13 across the lake. To our surprise and delight, Jim noticed a row boat tied to the bridge, and we trotted over to see who owned it. Since there was no one around, we spent some time inspecting this abandoned little craft. Finally, Jim, who said he had learned to pick locks by using different sized hair pins to open locked cabinets and chests around the house, suggested we use a couple of boards which were high and dry under the bridge to paddle ourselves on a short boat ride. Having learned from cowboy movies that picking locks on bank safes often resulted in time behind bars, I objected to actually picking the lock, but Jim convinced me that there was no one close enough to see us.

He had the pad lock off the mooring rope in a couple of minutes, and we were soon paddling merrily along the shore just north of the high way. We had just decided that we might take our new boat back to the camp sight to move our camp under the bridge in case of rain when an 18 foot cabin cruiser poked its nose from under the bridge where our boat had been moored. It came straight at us and pulled along side.

The pilot pulled a bottle of Stag beer from a cooler, snapped off the cap and said, "That boat belongs to George Hegler, a friend of mine. So, how did you kids get it?" It was time for some fast thinking, and one of us, I don't remember which, came up with what seemed a convincing answer.

"We found it drifting along close to the bank, so we grabbed the rope trailing behind it and was just getting ready to paddle around until we found the owner and gave it to him."

The guy took a long drink of Stag and said, "I'm goin' about a mile up the lake to run some trot lines. By the time I get back, that boat better have drifted back down to that bridge and tied itself up again, or you kids will be telling your story to the sheriff." He finished his beer, revved up his motor, tossed the bottle into our boat and sped off into a cove behind a tree-lined hill.

As the sound of the motor faded, the grass hoppers, crickets and other insects along the water's edge seemed to turn up their volume. Not wanting to renew our brief visit with the beer drinking fisherman, we made haste to paddle back to the bridge where we left the boat just like we found it and hurried back to the seclusion of our tree shrouded camp.

After swimming for a while, we went a way down the lake where we had bated a fishing line and found ourselves in possession of a small bass, which Jim cleaned for supper. Then, after sharing this very small meal cooked on our camp fire, we entertained ourselves by telling ghost stories and pretending I could hear and Jim could see various specters (such as the

Headless Horseman, Long John Silver, and Blue Beard) performing their blood curdling deeds just outside the flickering light of our camp fire. This mental parade of supernatural horrors so terrorized us that we scrambled up a small tree when the pounding of large hoofs thundered through the woods directly at us. When the monster, a spotted-hound about knee high, came to a sliding halt before the fire and began examining the skillet containing the crumbs of our dinner, we sheepishly descended from the tree and crawled into our bed rolls. Several times during the night, I thought I heard some one looting our camp, but it was always the spotted hound trying to scrape one more crumb of fish from the skillet.

The next sound that invaded my slumber was a heavy thud, which I subsequently learned was the sound of a log crashing into a large stump near the water's edge. Jim explained that he had found a straight section of fallen tree about five feet long and one foot thick which he had rolled down the bank to serve as a sort of raft which could keep us afloat as we drifted around the small cove where we were camped. Retrieving the skillet, which had been nuzzled into the weeds by the hound, who apparently decided to become a permanent member of our camp, I washed and scoured it with a sandstone before disinfecting it in the fire which Jim had rekindled. The bacon and potatoes fried in the clean skillet retained no taste of dog, and, invigorated by this hardy breakfast, we were soon using the buoyant log to cross and re-cross the narrow neck of water next to our camp.

The day went splendidly until about 2:00 O'clock. We had used our "raft" to fairy our gear across the cove as a part of a fantasy in which we pretended to be soldiers in Washington's Army stealthily crossing the Delaware River to capture the British Red Coats. Pretending to be Tom Sawyer and Huck Finn floating lazily down the Mississippi, we became aware of a brisk wind blowing from the shore. The sudden chill of the water told me that the sun had disappeared behind a cloud, or that we had drifted underneath a very tall tree. "Where are we?" I shouted at Jim.

The log jerked as he righted himself and said in a rather high-pitch voice, "We've drifted way the hell out in the lake, twice as far as we can swim!" In fact, neither of us could swim more than a few feet, preferring to kick our way around while supporting ourselves with an inner tube or piece of drift wood. If we did not take immediate action to return to the shore, we would soon find ourselves being blown into the middle of the lake, where drowning was a distinct possibility if the wind continued to increase.

Following some intense conversation as to how we could keep one end of the log aimed at the nearest land while propelling it toward shore against the wind resistance, we agreed that Jim, who could see to aim our craft at the nearest dry land, would lie on top of the log and kick water with all his might, making necessary course corrections by kicking harder with his right or left foot, while I remained almost submerged and tried to keep the log pointed into the wind. I must have asked Jim twenty times if the land looked any closer before my left big toe made contact with mud. Perhaps being just a little irritated because Jim never answered and had almost got us arrested by picking the lock on Mr. Hegler's boat yesterday, I had a sudden urge to give him a little scare. Instead of rising out of the water as it became more shallow, I began crouching down, keeping my nose just above the surface. After asking my question one last time, I yelled at the top of my voice, "Something's got my foot!" At the same instant, I twisted the log violently to the left, dumping Jim into what he thought was twenty feet of water inhabited by some under sea monster which could bite off his foot.

After ducking me in the lake a couple of times, Jim cooled down and finally began to laugh, saying it was a pretty good trick I played on him. While we were walking back to town that afternoon, he even said he thought we had really acted cool under pressure, "sort of like Roy Rogers who quieted a stampeding heard of cattle by singing to them at the movie last Saturday."

Mean while, back at PK's: the length of the story had emptied our glasses, and I was ready for a wash room break. Dee diverted my wash room trip with, "So, your point is that a sighted person must be lucky enough to share some quality time with one of these rare blind people in order to really know and accept that person?" Settling back on my stool, I replied that her statement applied to the formation of a relationship with any person, blind or sighted. "Well," she said with a smile in her voice, "since I have you to practice on and our mugs need filled, why don't you order another round so we can continue this noble experiment in the psychology of human relationships?" In the spirit of suspense and anticipation, the result of this "noble experiment" is left to the speculation of the reader.

Alvin Roberts

RIDE'EM, COWBOY

"What have you been up to?" asked Mop Head, settling on to the stool next to me and asking the bar tender to locate and fill his personal PK'S mug. Of course, Mop Head was a nick name coined by some one in his distant past because of his mop of shoulder-length blond hair, which ended in thick curls. Now, Mop Head is an outdoor, physically active guy who enjoys riding Harleys, basket ball, fishing and horse back riding. He explained that he was moving rather slowly because of a horse-back riding accident the previous week. Mop Head lives on a farm in the Shawnee Hills about twenty miles south-east of Carbondale, and one of his pastimes is riding through this rugged country side and feasting his eyes on aesthetically pleasing images such as the last rays of sun light climbing the eastern slope of a valley encompassing a farm house and a meandering creek. It was during one of these rides on what he described as the most gentle horse on the farm that Mop Head became involved in a potentially life-threatening accident. He never saw what spooked the palomino, possibly a snake, but the usually placid animal reared up and tumbled over backward down the steep hill he was ascending. Mop Head landed squarely under the horse, which quickly rolled off of him and stood near by shaking like he had seen a ghost. Mop Head made no immediate effort to move, partly because the fall had knocked the breath out of him and partly because he figured his ribs might be splintered, in which case movement might puncture a lung. To his surprise, he was able to breathe almost normally once his lungs re-inflated, and a digital examination of his rib cage seemed to reveal no serious brakes, perhaps a cracked rib or two. This diagnosis was confirmed by the local doctor, and Mop Head had lucked out with only severe bruises and a lot of pain. He attributed his good fortune to the tall saddle horn which kept some of the horse's weight off of him and his upper body landing to the left side of the horse.

15

This was his first trip to town since the accident, and he wanted to catch up on the news. I told of a recent work trip involving some interesting after-hour recreation such as an evening spent on the Alton Bell Casino, ending my little narrative by recounting a riding accident during my childhood which was almost identical to Mop Head's recent mishap. I never had adequate vision to drive motor vehicles; so I substituted horse back riding as a way to satisfy my adolescent need to drive cars like my peers. It was during one of these rides on a rather spirited plow horse that I reined in too harshly, causing the animal to rear up. Riding bare-back, my feet were not encumbered by stirrups. When the horse began to pump its front legs in the air, I pushed off hard to the right, landing with a thud in the gravel. Although the gravel inflicted considerable skins and bruises, the horse fell in the other direction. It was on its feet before I had stopped rolling and I knew I had a long, painful walk coming when its hoof beats faded away in the direction of our farm.

Mop Head reckoned as how he might have also been able to throw himself from under his horse if he had been riding bare back, but he was still grateful that the saddle did keep the entire weight from crushing him. The conversation turned to childhood exploits, and I related the following adventure in some detail, after making a short trip to the wash room and ordering up another round.

About a year after the attack on Pearl Harbor pushed the United States into World War II, my mother, stepfather and I moved to a farm about one mile north of Carbondale, Illinois. Up until this move, I had always lived just a few houses from my cousin, Jim, who was two years younger than I. Jim and I did almost everything together: sleeping and eating at each others homes, acting out all sorts of fantasies based on cowboy and war movies, fighting with kids from other neighborhoods, and doing home work. Being blind, I was not attending school at the time; so Jim helped me convince the fourth grade teacher at Lincoln School that I could participate in her class with some reading by him and other students. On the afternoon of December seventh, 1941, Jim and I were studying our spelling lesson at a friend's house when an official sounding voice on the radio informed us of the Japanese attack. It all sounded very much like the war movies we had been acting out, and we were excited about being in a real war. When we ran home to tell my mother of the exciting news and how we were willing and ready to become war heroes, her response was extremely discouraging. She said that we were thoughtless kids to be happy about a war in which many people, including our own family members, might be killed. She, forthwith, chased us out of her kitchen with a broom, and told us not to show our faces again until dinner, by which time we would be expected to act like sensible children.

My stepfather did not become a war hero, but he did perform a valuable service in support of our troops. After a few months working in a defense plant, he decided to use his considerable knowledge of horses and farming to supply draft animals to local farmers, who were substituting work horses for tractors in order to conserve fuel which was needed at the battle front. To engage in this enterprise, we moved to the farm north of town, which had a barn large enough to accommodate at least fifteen horses and mules. This barn was so large that three abandoned box cars had been detached from their wheels and built in for use as corn cribs and tack rooms. My stepfather would buy young horses and train them to pull plows, farm wagons and other machinery, after which he would sell them to local farmers. A portion of this training was the plowing of Victory Gardens tended by store owners, bankers, college professors, house wives and other patriotic citizens. In this way, he was able to make a double contribution to the war effort while earning a comfortable income for our little family. At one dollar for plowing a small plot in a victory gardener's back yard, he was able to earn about fifteen dollars a day, approximately three times the average wage.

During the summer, he often allowed Jim and me to assist him by feeding and watering the horses, helping with the loading and unloading of utensils as we moved from one garden plot to another, and circulating among the neighbors while he was plowing a particular plot to solicit jobs from other patriotic gardeners. It was only natural that we would incorporate the knowledge gained from this experience into our recreational pursuits. Our experience in riding a variety of plow horses led to speculation about our abilities to participate in various wild west adventures, such as taming wild horses and riding long horn bulls in rodeos. At first, we pretended the work horses in our charge were wild mustangs which we were breaking for the U. S. Cavalry, but the most action we could get from these critters after a day's plowing was a slow gallop; so, we began to cast about for a more challenging beast to tame.

One rainy day when we had exhausted our resources for acting out various wild west scenarios, Jim looked at a yearling calf peaceably munching hay from a manger in a corridor which ran the length of the barn. "That looks like the wild bull we seen a cow boy riding in the rodeo held at the carnival grounds last month," observed Jim. When I protested that this was a scrawny calf with no horns, Jim said the coloring was right, and, besides, good acting depended on a little imagination, which I was not using. I finally agreed to work at adopting the right frame of mind for creating a rodeo ring out of a long barn entry way, but I knew it was going to stretch my imagination to its fullest in order to make this pet calf into a raging, long-horn bull. This friendly creature would eat corn out of my hand and was willing to be led by a rope looped around its neck. Jim enhanced the feeling of a closed rodeo ring by closing the gates at each end of the corridor, but there was not much he could do about changing the personality of the calf.

We had no difficulty in leading our newly created long-horn into a narrow passageway between the corn crib and an opened door at the east end of the barn. This narrow space was to be the shoot out of which would emerge the brave rodeo rider on the bucking bull. It was decided that I would take the first turn since I was acquainted with the animal. Using the heels of my boots to locate the rungs of the ladder leading to the hay loft, I backed two steps up the wall and swung my left leg over the calf. Expecting the calf to come out of the shoot like a bullet, I locked my legs around its ribs as tight as possible and locked my hands on its neck. The only action was the calf turning its head around to sniff at my foot. "What's wrong with him?" shouted Jim from the ladder somewhere above me. I bounced a couple of times to encourage some action, but my steed did not even take a step. Jim came down the ladder, grasped the calf by the ears and tried to lead it from its secure space behind the barn door. When this strategy failed, he brought a leather strap from the tack room, climbed a few steps up the ladder, and smacked the animal sharply across the rump, yelling, "Ride'em, cow boy!" The yearling shot forward, spraying manure and gas. To my astonishment, I stayed on, probably because the frightened beast was running instead of bucking. After about ten steps, my hat was whisked off, the calf came to a quick stop, and I continued in a straight projectory until my progress was blocked by the closed gate at the west end of the barn.

Picking myself up very slowly, I determined that I had sustained no real injuries, with the exception of a small scratch on the top of my head. It was so quiet in the barn that I thought Jim had run outside to escape the manure spewed by the calf. After a long silence, Jim said, "I don't think this rodeo game is very safe. We better quit before your step dad gets back and tans our hides." I reminded him that my step father never punished me and suggested that we would find another activity after he had one turn on the "bull". Jim said that he had lost all interest in bull riding. When I protested that fairness required that he not be denied a turn, Jim took me to the west end of the barn and had me reach up to where a two by six inch brace protruded from the wall. My hat was hanging on a spike which had removed it from my head as the calf passed under it.

"If you hadn't had your head down trying to hold on to the calf's neck, that nail would have went right through your eye. I could see everything from the ladder," Jim informed me. My

19

knees got weak when I imagined that spike piercing my head. It had been close enough to part my hair, and that was too close. We decided to release our pet calf, which resumed its munching, and went to the house for some lemonade. There after we confined our interest in bull riding to the Saturday afternoon movies.

"BOTTLE" GAP

"Generation gap" is one of those cliches used to explain everything from differences in food preference to expressions of distaste by many older persons for the publication of intimate sexual presidential grand jury testimony on the internet. To experience the magnitude of this phrase for people living at the beginning of the twenty-first century, we need only observe interactions between parents in their late thirties and their teen age children. "Ma, you're too old to appreciate modern music because you grew up with those funky songs of the 1980's," or, "Kids have not worn those old-fashion clothes to school since way back in 1993," are statements by my teen-age granddaughters to their mothers which graphically illustrate the shrinking period of years mentally dividing one generation from another. This process of generation shrinking has been rapidly accelerating since the beginning of the industrial revolution when each new generation began using tools and appliances unknown to their parents, traveling farther and faster than their fore-bearers, and receiving information from around the globe more and more rapidly. We tend to accept the world of our childhood as permanent and reliable, something we never had to "adjust to," an environment as natural and comfortable as our own back yards. Totally new technology and drastic shifts in life styles occurring after our formative years seem foreign and intrusive to our comfortable existence. If, in the year, 2010, a device to interpret thoughts by analyzing brain waves is marketed, it will seem as foreign and intrusive to our grand children as the invasion of privacy made possible through computer technology seems to those of us educated with print books, type writers and slide rules.

My grandmother was an intelligent, resourceful, aggressive woman born in the 1880's, but she began to experience a real generation gap after she stopped working and moved back to the small town of her childhood. She continued to do things the way she had always done them, working in her garden, baking delicious pies and bread, and telling stories to her grand children. She limited her reading to the local paper which concentrated on local events such as who was entertaining out-of-town guests, marriage and funeral announcements. She really did not care for the radio because the closest station was about twenty miles away and did not report news of her town. All of this is not meant to imply that Grandma was out of step with or considered eccentric by her neighbors. In fact, relatives and friends often remarked on her knowledge of distant places (such as St. Louis and Chicago) where she had traveled with her third husband, who was a bridge construction foreman for the Illinois Central Railroad. She also displayed interest in electricity, often observing classes conducted by her son Thomas to acquaint local youth with the safe use of electric power which was just becoming available in rural areas in the late 1930's. These classes were sponsored by the National Youth Administration following the enactment of the Rural Electrification Act and were conducted in a small frame building which Grandma had built behind her house for this purpose. She would often reward Thomas's aspiring electricians with refreshments during the break and remain to observe work on their projects, such as replacing fuses, building miniature electric motors or coil radio receivers. The generation or technology gap between small town people like Grandma and others in urban areas was a result of different rates of new product distribution and information dissemination. Except for the replacement of the horse by the automobile, the kerosene lamp by the incandescent light, and the advent of the phonograph and radio, very little change had occurred in the everyday life of rural America between Grandma's birth in the 1880's and the 1930's and 1940's. True, these were major changes, but Grandma had the luxury of a fifty-year period to integrate these new-fangled contraptions into her life style.

When she first moved back to her home town of Sesser, Grandma would anticipate visits to the much larger town of

Carbondale, where she had resided with her third husband, Logan Turner, from the late 1920's to the mid 1930's. Whereas she had enjoyed the diversity created by students attending Southern Illinois Normal, a teachers' college, and the variety of people drawn to the area to work on the Illinois Central Railroad, she soon began to space her visits further and further apart. The bustle of the larger community seemed somehow to confuse her, and she eventually wanted to get back to her own town after only a day or two. In time, she would request to be taken home within hours of her arrival, stating she needed to be home by dark.

Once, after an absence of about two years, my mother persuaded Grandma to come for an extended visit of several days. This was after the conclusion of world War II, and the pent-up demand for new products had produced a flurry of invention and manufacturing of new gadgets to enable the house wives of America to retain much of the freedom they had achieved by joining the defense workforce during the Great War. It was during this short visit that Grandma ran head-long into the generation gap. It wasn't that she opposed women working outside the home. She had worked as a cook for her husband's bridge building crew who lived in railway cars which were moved from one construction site to another, but she was dependent on coal stoves and kerosene lamps, while my Mom, by the early 1950's, was managing a restaurant with electric appliances and air conditioning. If we had thought of the startling effect which some of the jew gadgets in our home would have on Grandma, I am certain Mom would have taken more time to explain and demonstrate them to her.

The first disturbing gadget Grandma encountered was the pop-up toaster. She arrived at our house just before lunch, and Mom asked her to remove and butter the toast while I brought in the mail and Mom set the table. When a yell emanated from the kitchen, we rushed in to find Grandma holding a dish towel above the toaster. She explained that the toast had been ejected with such force that she feared the next pieces would be hurled on to the floor. So, after placing the first batch on a plate, she inserted two cold slices of bread and was holding the towel in position in case the machine threw the second batch harder than the first. During the remainder of her visit, she stood with a towel poised to catch the flying toast when ever the pop-up was in use.

Another phenomenon which Grandma found difficult to understand was how her voice could be captured on a tape. Although she had owned a spring-driven phonograph for many years, she had never seen a recording made. We turned on the reel-to-reel recorder one evening and encouraged Grandma to talk about her past. At first she thought the play back was a recording of her sister Martha. "It's too young sounding for me!" she asserted. After several brief recordings with immediate play-back of her voice, she agreed it was really her. But having observed that, somehow, the music emanating from a recorded disk was stored in the grooves, she could not understand how sound could be stored on a tape without some kind of embossing or, at least, marks.

Grandma was surprised by several other new inventions during her visit including an automatic can opener, the magnetic seal on the refrigerator door, and an automatic door at the local grocery store. "Don't that beat all! The door seems to know you have your arms full and opens even before you touch the knob," she pondered. The event which disturbed her most and probably caused Grandma to cut her visit short, occurred on the third day of her visit, just before lunch. Grandma and I were alone. Both my mother and stepfather were at work, and I had been helping Grandma re-pot some flowers which had outgrown their containers. About eleven-thirty, she asked me to run across the alley to Weese's Grocery for some lunch meat and milk. After returning with a roll of bologna and a half gallon of milk in one of the new waxed card board cartons, which was replacing the glass bottle, I went into the living room to listen to Lucky Leroy, a country singer who advertised local businesses on WCIL Radio at 11:30 A. M.. Leroy was just starting "The singing news" when

I heard Grandma scream, "Lord, help me!" Thinking that she had cut herself while slicing the bologna, I leaped from my comfortable rocking chair and bounded into the kitchen. Slipping in a puddle of liquid, I ended up on my back under the table. While helping me to my feet, she explained that I had slipped in the milk. Grandma was very sorry and embarrassed to explain that, thinking there was a glass bottle of milk inside the card board container, she had cut it open with a butcher knife. After cleaning up the kitchen, Grandma sent me for another "cardboard bottle" of milk. While we were eating lunch, she asked me not to mention this last encounter with the new gadgets, and, that evening, she asked Mom if someone could drive her home the next morning, explaining that she was concerned about an elderly neighbor and that her garden needed watering. After that, Grandma seldom visited, preferring that we come to her house.

Alvin Roberts

STASHING THE CASH

A recurring conversation theme among those of us courteously referred to as "Senior citizens" is the comparison of the high prices of today with the low cost of goods and services in "The good old days." All it takes to set me off on a lecture extolling the responsible attitude toward money demonstrated by my generation is for one of my grandchildren to say, during a shopping trip to Walmart, "Grandpa! This toy only costs $5, and you have lots of money." Just as I launch into my speech about $5 being more than my father made in a week during the 1930's, the bored child usually disappears into the next aisle to admire a more interesting and costly item. Often these incidents serve as examples to illustrate the cavalier attitude of the younger generation toward saving for the future when we old folks get together at social functions. One such discussion occurred recently at the 1999 Convention of the Illinois Council of the Blind, a special interest group devoted to the improvement of employment opportunities, education and the over-all quality of life for people who are blind.

The banquet was over, and several of us gathered in the Clarion Hotel room occupied by Bryce and Helen Huddleston for a night cap and a critique of the banquet speeches. The youngest person in the room was at least fifty years old. The high cost of banquet meals and hotel accommodations was cited as a sound reason for holding this convention in Champaign rather than Chicago, where the going price for a room exceeded $100 per night. Bryce pointed out that the room rate in such fine hotels as the Sherman House in Chicago was between $6 and $10 a night in 1960, which is an increase of more than 1000 percent in the past forty years. Someone mentioned that a pack of cigarettes has shown a similar increase from 30 cents in 1960 to $3 in 1999. I reported buying a 1963 Rambler car with 25,000 miles on the odometer in 1965 for $900; a Ford escort with 17,000 miles cost me $9,000 in 1993, also a 1000 percent increase. We continued amusing ourselves with such price comparisons for some time when someone-- it may have been Joanna Cargill— told of a friend who had discovered a cash of old coins inside a brick wall during the remodeling of a home built shortly after the Great Depression by an eccentric banker who had lost heavily on the stock market in 1929 and wanted some hard currency available in case history repeated itself.

This line of conversation reminded me of an amusing incident involving my stepfather, Buck Brewer. Buck was a gregarious, fun-loving character who enjoyed drinking and story telling with his friends when he was not conducting his small contracting business, trading horses or doctoring livestock. He was also an avid reader of pulp westerns. A retired cowboy, Dan Batson, operated a cowboy book store in the big living room of his old two-story house just a few doors south of our home, and Buck would trade Dan two westerns for one he had not read. Dan would sell these for a nickel each to readers who had no trades. Since it took two books to trade for one he had not read, Buck often had to cough up a nickel to replenish his reading material.

It was one of these western tales which Buck incorporated into real life that became the punch line of this story. A favorite pastime of Buck and his friends was to gather at a long table in the rear of Big Charlie's saloon and try to out-do each other in the telling of tall tales. This "literary" gathering occurred several times a week after work, but the marathon sessions were reserved for Saturdays when the participants were not required to work the following day. Gandi, the bar tender, once remarked that these yarn spinners seemed most eloquent and enthusiastic when rain or snow provided them with an excuse to spend an entire day drinking, playing pranks on each other, and telling jokes and outlandish yarns. Over time, Buck perfected the technique of weaving events from some of his stories in Western Weekly and other "literary" sources into yarns about himself, his friends and family. This technique often made Buck's stories stand out from those of others in the group in terms of excitement and suspense. Occasionally, one of the yarn spinners would chide Buck with the assertion that he had read a very similar account in a cowboy story. Buck would usually reply that he might have borrowed a thing or two from a "shoot-em-up western" and then justify his plagiarism with, "But, didn't that little twist make it one hell of a yarn?"

One March day in 1939, a cold rain driven by an icy, north wind caused men working in the fields around Carbondale, Illinois to abandon their plows, mules, shovels and other tools and converge on Big Charlie's saloon for warmth, food, drink, and fellowship. Watt Glenn, the road commissioner, was the first to arrive. In fact, he came straight from his breakfast where he learned from his radio that rain, and possibly snow, was on the way. Generally, Watt's favorite drink was coffee, although he might consume two or three beers or glasses of wine during a long day of yarn swopping, at which pastime he rivaled Buck in holding the interest of the crowd. Next, came Jeff Dillinger, then Marion Holiday, and Bill Swendel. Buck showed up about ten o'clock and bought a drink for the house, which had grown to about thirty drenched laborers in need of some warming alcoholic spirits.

The workers enjoyed their weather enforced holiday with their usual array of pastimes. After everyone was thoroughly thawed-out by the heat from the steam radiators and a couple of drinks, most partook of a hearty plate lunch from Big Charlie's lunch counter: pork steak or fried chicken, mashed potatoes with white gravy, mustard greens, corn bread and raisin pie. Afterward, several revelers occupied themselves with a penny-a-point pinochle game while a few played checkers, and the others entertained themselves by telling stories and jokes. Watt told of an old time horse trader who applied brown paint to convert an ancient gray horse into a pinto pony and sold it for an exorbitant price just before a hard rain. When the paint washed off, the irate purchaser and some friends caught the deceptive trader, extracted the purchase price (plus enough for a round of drinks), and would have hung the man by his heels from a beam in Sam

Enderson's livery stable if the town marshal had not put an end to the festivities. There were several jokes about the proverbial traveling salesman and the farmer's daughter. Buck narrated an incident from his childhood in which a boyhood friend, who had placed a bucket over his head to entice a goat to engage in a game of "bull fight," had his head driven into the bucket by the charging goat. Watt told a fascinating tale, which he attributed to the famous western writer Bret Harte. The yarn was about a gambler who was so worried about being robbed of his winnings that he hid his money in his stove. When he returned to his cabin, someone had built a roaring fire. Bucked enjoyed this yarn so much that he bought another drink for the house, which then contained only a dozen or so persistent partiers, the more sober men having wisely reported home for dinner. The enthusiasm of the remaining partiers made up for their diminished numbers. Many more stories were told and many more rounds were drunk.

About midnight, Buck staggered to his Model A truck and drove home. As he quietly entered through the kitchen, it suddenly occurred to him that he was carrying the payroll for his construction laborers, about $200, give or take a few dollars spent at Big Charlie's place. He knew that, once asleep, it would take a cyclone to wake him. What if someone picked his pocket while he was asleep? He would have to mortgage his truck and horses to make his payroll. Then, he remembered Watt's story about the gambler (at least the part about hiding the money in the stove). He wrapped the roll of bills in a handkerchief to keep them away from the dirt inside the cook stove and carefully placed the wad on top of the coal in the stove and closed the lid. Soon after quietly slipping into bed, Buck was snoring loud enough to wake the dead, according to my mother, who had been feigning sleep while surreptitiously observing the concealment of the money in her cook stove.

Mom was up early and had a roaring fire in the cook stove. She was removing a pan of hot, flaky biscuits from the oven when Buck stepped through the kitchen door and froze. Finally, he was able to speak in a hoarse, questioning voice, "Where did you put the money?"

When she had placed the biscuits, one by one, in a neat pyramid on a platter, Mom gave Buck a blank stare, and asked, "What money?" Although Buck insisted that she could not have missed seeing the roll of bills when she opened the stove to light the fire, Mom steadfastly maintained that there was no money in the stove when she removed the lid. Buck finally gave up questioning her and ate breakfast in silence. While he was dressing for work in the bed room, Mom stepped out the back door and tossed the handkerchief containing the pay roll on to the truck seat. When Buck opened the truck door and picked up the handkerchief, he was even more perplexed, insisting that he clearly remembered hiding his money in the stove just as Watt had described in the Bret Harte story, but Mom would have none of it. She repeatedly admonished that he was too drunk to know what he had done and demanded that he curtail his visits to Big Charlie's Saloon.

Alvin Roberts

THE DAY CHARLIE PRESERVED OLD GLORY

A plate of steaming food materialized on the bar before me, and the voice of Gwyn Hunt, owner of PK's, announced, "Polish sausage is at twelve o'clock, rice and beans at three o'clock, and your bread is at nine." Every Thursday, about 5:30 P.M. she sets up a small buffet at the end of the bar, and all the patrons are welcome to eat their fill at no cost. It is her way of expressing appreciation to her regular customers. Like several others who live alone, I grew to anticipate going straight from work to PK's for a meal and a little socializing once a week. Gwyn has been in business since the early 1960's, first as a proprietor of a pizza parlor named Pizza King, later shortened to PK's when her establishment stopped serving pizza and became a neighborhood tavern which served light lunch. Probably because I am blind and might stab someone with a fork in trying to spear a polish sausage from the buffet, Gwyn always fills my plate and informs me of the location of each item as though the plate were a clock face.

On this particular winter evening, she reappeared on the stool to my left with her plate of food, and we began to reminisce about people we had known during our 35-year friendship. My two daughters had gone through school with her two youngest daughters, and we had socialized together over the years, sharing many experiences, friends and acquaintances. Both Gwyn's daughter Kendra and my wife Cathy had been fatally stricken with brain aneurisms, and we often shared our common grief. On this snowy evening, however, the conversation turned to our extended relationship with Charlie Overton. Charlie was one of a kind. Some of his exploits were recounted in <u>Tavern Tales</u>, a collection of short stories which I published in 1993, but, as Gwyn reminded me that evening, I had omitted one of Charlie's most amusing adventures from <u>Tavern Tales</u>, copies of which are displayed for sale behind the bar. The omitted yarn was how Charlie saved the American Flag from desecration. But I'm getting ahead of myself. To derive maximum amusement from this little known act of heroic bravado, it is necessary to have some understanding of Charlie's unique view of his world and how he reacted to challenging situations.

Charlie Overton came to Carbondale, Illinois with his mother and stepfather in the 1930's and continued to reside in this community until his death in the mid 1970's, except for those periods when he was off on one of his adventures. These extended journeys began in the 1930's with hobo trips to such places as Arkansas, an adventure which was recounted in Tavern Tails entitled "The Happy Hobos". Charlie and his buddies would often be away for months, riding the rails, living in hobo camps and working in seasonal occupations such as fruit picking and wheat thrashing. On one occasion, he spent six months working on the construction of an air field in Alaska, but, as he aged, Charlie tended to keep his trips limited to Illinois and neighboring states, where he practiced the unusual trade of flag pole painting. Somewhere in his ramblings across America, Charlie apprenticed himself to a flag pole painter and learned how to tie a slip knot in a rope which became tighter with increasing tension. Somehow, he was able to anchor himself at a given spot on a slick flag pole, loosen the tension on the loop and cast it several feet higher on the pole, again tighten the loop and pull himself up to it. In this way, Charlie could ascend a fifty-foot pole with a can of paint strapped on his back in a very few minutes. On reaching the top of the pole, he would rest long enough for a cigarette, open the can and use the paint brush attached by a cord to his wrist to paint his way down the pole. Charlie charged a dollar a foot for this painting, and he could easily earn $150 a day. Generally he contacted school principles and other proprietors of public buildings in advance so he could plan his trips, procure paint and other supplies and complete the jobs each day. In time, these officials began to anticipate his schedule, and all Charlie had to do was send a post card notifying each of them of the date and approximate time he would arrive. Although Charlie did most of this work during the summer, the increased demand for his services eventually caused him to paint some poles in the late Spring or early Autumn when school was in session. On such occasions, the students were often so fascinated with Charlie's flag pole painting routine that little learning occurred during his visits, and, in a few instances, the principle interrupted classes so the students could gather on the lawn and watch. At some point, Charlie began to spend a few moments telling the students about the symbolic importance of the American flag. At first his speeches were very short because of his limited knowledge of the tradition surrounding the flag, but trips to the public library began to expand his speeches into such topics as the creation of our first flag by Betsy Ross, the writing of our national anthem by Francis Scott Key, who was inspired by his vision of the flag flying over Baltimore Harbor during the War of 1812, and the proper care and display of "Old Glory." Long after his flag painting days were passed, and Charlie was doing odd jobs such as cleaning up PK'S bar, he enjoyed telling patrons how he had educated a generation of school children to respect and care for the American flag.

May 4, 1970 was the day Charlie encountered a situation which challenged him to perform the very procedures for displaying the flag with reverence and patriotism which he had so often described to groups of attentive school children. At first, the customers in PK'S had watched quietly as the pictures of injured and dying students at the Kent State University riot flashed across the television behind the bar. In the beginning, their expressions were blank or disbelieving, but, as the film was repeatedly shown and the commentators revealed that at least four students had been shot by the National Guard, their expressions ranged from horror and sorrow to outright hostility. As the image of President Nixon appeared on the screen to express condolences for the tragedy and explain his reasons for expanding the war in Vietnam (which precipitated the riots), angry accusations were shouted at the TV. Someone tossed a piece of gum which adhered to the image of the American flag that appeared on the screen as the President finished his statement. Charlie, who had been watching intensely, left his stool, removed the gum with a tissue, and shouted to someone down the bar, "No matter how much you hate the war, you have no right to desecrate the American flag." After exchanging some heated words with this customer, Charlie was persuaded to resume his seat at the bar by Gwyn Hunt who poured him a free beer. As the crowd both inside and outside the bar became more agitated and belligerent, Charlie continued to sip his beer and quietly observe the scene around him. However, when the crowd began to applaud a TV segment in which several young adults were cutting an American flag into strips and stamping on them, Charlie leapt to his feet and strode out the front door shouting, "It's time to teach you jerks a little respect for Old Glory, and, by god, I'm just the man to teach you." The situation continued to deteriorate. Gwyn was kept busy meeting the increased demand for drinks as the crowd became more unruly. About 8:00 P.M., a customer shouted across the bar, "You'll never believe what's going on next door at the Ward's Store! That old skinny, grey-haired guy that cleans up the bar is climbing up the front of the building with an American flag." Asking an off-duty bartender to take over, Gwen rushed outside just in time to see Charlie swing himself from a drain pipe to the top of the Ward building and begin tying the flag to the flashing neon sign. Just as he looped the tie chord around a rod supporting the sign, a strong wind gust stretched the flag to its full display position and Charlie lost his grip on the chord. The flag sailed proudly across Illinois Avenue and dropped ignominiously into an open trash can. One of the demonstrators, a girl wearing a tee shirt with the words, "Kill the pigs!", on the front, retrieved the flag and began to stomp it into the dirt. A male demonstrator was preparing to urinate on the flag when Charlie, who had descended the drain pipe in record time, hit him from behind. Snatching the flag from the girl, he quickly disappeared into the crowd, which was converging on the spot where the flag had fallen. The next word Gwyn had of Charlie was the report of a police officer who informed her that he was in jail and needed one-hundred dollars bail. The story was that the police had discovered him burning a flag in an alley.

When the money was pledged and Charlie returned to the bar, he explained that he had to appear in court the following week, and needed his freedom in order to collect evidence to prove his innocence. When the Court appointment day came, Charlie did not appear at PK'S as usual to perform odd jobs and mingle with the other patrons. In fact, Gwyn felt a little put out with him because she had to send one of the children to run errands, such as picking up a can of coffee from Spires Grocery, and she had to run to the bank for change, which left the bar unattended for about ten minutes.

Just after the last customer had paid for lunch and the bar was nearly vacant, Charlie strolled through the front door, swaggered up to the bar and ceremoniously placed a large, white book before Gwyn. "There it is," he announced, "exhibit number one. I showed this baby to the judge, and it clenched my case. He didn't even sentence me to sweep out the court room." One of the remaining customers, who had been present when the flag was dropped from the neon sign, ordered Charlie a frosty mug of beer and asked him what happened at court that morning. "Not much til the judge called me," Charlie explained. "The other cases were routine. One guy got fined $200 for disorderly conduct, and another one was let off for wife beating. The judge reasoned that the husband, who looked like he had tangled with Mohamad Ali, was the looser in the fight because the wife didn't have a bruise on her."

"My case, on-the-other-hand, dealt with a fundamental issue of the United States Constitution, according to the judge. He said flag burning might well be a violation of the First Amendment, and that's heavy duty stuff."

"How come you're walkin' around free as a bird, drinkin' free beer, then?" asked the customer who order both him and Charlie another mug.

Charlie continued his narration of the morning court session. "Well, the judge reads out my full name, Charles Harvey

Overton, and orders me to tell the truth, the whole truth and nothing but the truth. Then, this County Prosecutor asks me a lot of little questions, adding up to the big one: did I pour gas on the flag and burn it in the alley behind the feed store? Well, I had to answer yes to every question because I said I would tell the truth. But, when that old boy tried to get me to say that I burned that flag because I hated the Government and wanted to destroy the symbol of the United States, we had a powerful disagreement. He tried for about twenty minutes to trick me into agreeing with his statements that I burned the flag because I hated the war, hated the CIA, the FBI, or several other things. Finally, the judge called a halt, and asked me why I did burn the flag. This was just the question I had been trying to answer all the time that prosecutor was shouting that I had to answer only yes or no."

Charlie then said he placed the white book, Volume 6 of the World Book Encyclopedia, 1957, which was lying on the bar opened to page 2587, before the judge and asked him to read the section on: "How to Care for the Flag."

The Judge adjusted his glasses and read: "The flag may be mended, washed or dry cleaned. When the flag has become so badly soiled or ragged that it is no longer a fitting emblem for display, it should be destroyed privately in a dignified way, preferably by burning." Charlie stated that it may have been possible to mend the flag, but it was his opinion that the attempts of the demonstrators to stamp it into the mud and urinate on it had soiled the flag to where it was "no longer a fitting emblem". Therefore, he had found a private place and destroyed the flag, except for the piece the policeman had retrieved.

Charlie said the judge was quiet for a long time, and then he said, "Mr. Overton, you have shown good citizenship in trying to care for the flag in a dignified manner. I am sure the police officer was sincere in the performance of his duty when he interrupted you in doing your duty as a United States citizen. I am returning the unburned section of the flag and ordering you and the arresting officer to return to the alley and complete the flag burning ceremony."

PART TWO

Stories from my Neighbor's Bar Stool

Alvin Roberts

PLANTIN' OLD BUCK

Walley held the beer mug up to the light in order to assure himself that no trace of lipstick or other residue had survived his perfunctory wash job and placed it on a tray behind the bar to air dry. "Clean enough for you?" asked Sloupek from his perch on a stool at the end of the L-shaped bar.

"It don't particularly concern me whether it's cleaned or not, since I drink my beer out of a bottle. It's guys like you that drink out of glasses that need to worry about whether I get off all the crud and germs," said Walley, continuing his glass washing and inspection routine.

"How come you got so many dirty glasses, anyhow?" Sloupek inquired.

"Ladies Auxiliary meetin' last night, and you know them gals can't drink anything out of a bottle or can. They left lipstick on every glass in the place," complained Walley.

About that time, several other patrons of the Carbondale American Legion came in, and Walley was kept busy filling drink orders for a few minutes. John took the stool to Sloupek's right so he could keep an eye on the TV mounted at the other end of the long leg of the L-shaped bar while participating in the conversation going on up and down the bar. It didn't matter to John that the TV sound was turned off. The movie, "Fighting C.B.'s," was a rerun he had seen many times but still enjoyed watching the action as John Wayne led his construction battalion in building bridges and other military installations under enemy fire. Observing John's attention to the silent TV screen, Sloupek asked, "How in the hell can you tell what's goin' on with no sound and these guys yakking their heads off up and down the bar?" John said he had watched the movie with sound many times, and then explained that he still liked to see the action because it reminded him of friends who had served in the C.B.'s during World War II. If he had been old enough, John thought, he would have liked to have served in the C.B.'s.

Some one about half way down the bar said he had a relative killed while building an air strip on the Island of Guam during "The Big War". Several patrons mentioned friends and relatives lost in World War II, Korea, or Vietnam. Next, the conversation turned to reminiscences of Legion members who had died of, more or less, natural causes after completion of military service. Hank Highland, Gib Black, Bill Cargill, Al Casper, Walkey-Talkey (whose real name no one could recall): all were remembered with a personal characteristic or story, often humorous, which those present readily associated with these deceased comrades. Finally, they began trying to remember who had served in the honor guards or as pallbearers for deceased members.

All this time, Walley continued to serve drinks and wash glasses. About 3:00 in the afternoon, Walley was telling about how Bill Cargill, who raised and sold vegetables, would come into the club on Saturday afternoons and brag on the size and quality of his produce (which would improve drastically as afternoon passed into evening). Charlie Downen swung through the door, shaking water from his coat. "It's rainin' like a cow pissin' on a flat rock out there" exclaimed Charlie. He draped his jacket over a chair to dry and pulled himself on to a stool to the left of Sloupek, who offered to buy him a beer. "Have to wait till my teeth stop chatterin'," mumbled Charlie. Walley asked Charlie if he remembered how Bill used to go on about raising the best vegetables in Makanda township. "Yeah! According to Bill, them tomatoes was the size of grape fruit when he would come into the club, but they would grow to the size of cantaloupes by the time he left that night."

Stooping to fish a beer out of the cooler for Charlie, Walley mused, "You older guys remember another fellow that used to tell some tall tales was Buck Brewer. He didn't come in here very often. In fact, I don't think Buck was ever in the service."

"Buck hung out over at Jim MacDaniel's Tavern and Bill's Tavern," Charlie filled in. One of the older vets informed the group that Bill's Tavern, which was located on what is now the parking lot for the ABC Liquor Store, was known as Big Charlie's Place in the nineteen-thirties.

"Not to be confused with Charlie Downen," cautioned Walley.

"I think that Charlie came from Christopher," said Charlie Downen. "I came to Carbondale from Sesser," he continued, "but let me tell you a funny story about Buck Brewer. It's Buck's last story."

Charlie began. "It has to do with his funeral. You see, several of us guys were over at Jim MacDaniel's Tavern one rainy afternoon in the fall of 1953. Jim Mac himself came in and told Jeff, who was tending bar, to set up a round of drinks on the house because he had some bad news to tell us, and a little liquid refreshment might make this bad news go down a little better. After the dozen or so of us standing along the bar had been served, Jim said, 'Boys, we've lost a good friend, one that's been around this town all of his life and has provided employment for most of you at one time or another.' He went on to tell us that Buck died in Holden Hospital the previous night. Somebody asked how long Buck had ben in the hospital, and Jim said he was only in there for about an hour. The way Jim heard it from one of the boys who worked for Joe VanNatta (a local undertaker) as an ambulance driver, he and his buddy were called to pick up a sick person from an apartment located above Wisely's Florist in the four hundred block of South Illinois Avenue at about ten P.M. the previous night. To their surprise, the sick man was Buck Brewer, who had been seen about town only a few days before. The thing that made the situation even more surprising was that Buck called them by name and asked if they would be busy in about an hour. The driver told Buck that he couldn't say where he would be in an hour because that depended on who needed an ambulance and where they were at. Buck answered that his doctor wanted him to come to the hospital for treatment, but they could save a little time and gasoline if they could wait around the hospital for an hour and then deliver him to the Vannatta Funeral Home. The boys

43

assured Buck that the Doc would have him on his feet in a few days, and no more was said about the matter. They unloaded Buck at the ambulance entrance and went about their business."

"What happened to poor old Buck?" asked Jeff, the bar tender, who was finding it necessary to wipe his eyes with his bar apron. "Why did he die so fast?"

Jim resumed by telling them that things happened just like Buck said they would. About midnight, the ambulance was called to take Buck to VanNatta's Funeral Home. Jim didn't know much more about Buck's death, except that he and others had noticed Buck's health failing for about the past year. It seemed to have something to do with his stomach. Jim had noticed that Buck was not holding his liquor very well. He would become drunk after only three or four shots of whisky--which was not at all like Buck. Beer seemed to make him short of breath. That was about all Jim could tell us, except that Joe VanNatta had asked for six of Buck's friends--some of the boys who had worked for him on construction jobs-, if possible, to serve as pallbearers. Since the funeral was to be the next day, most of us decided to go home early so as to be in good shape to say "good bye" to our old friend." Charlie accepted another beer which Walley placed before him and continued his story.

About 1:30 the next afternoon, the pallbearers gathered around Joe VanNatta for instructions on how to deliver Buck to his final resting place. Joe drew little maps of how we would move the coffin from the funeral chapel and role it into the hearse on rollers located inside the vehicle. He said this was an unusually difficult funeral because we would have to take the coffin out of the hearse and hall it about a quarter of a mile to the cemetery in a horse-drawn wagon. This maneuver was necessary because the dirt road was in bad condition. Several days of rain had filled the ruts with water and turned the flat surfaces into soft mud. Joe wasn't even sure the wagon could make it to the grave site.

It was still raining when they got to the end of the gravel road, where we were to transfer the coffin to the wagon. One of the pallbearers-- Clarence Bennet--remarked that Buck would probably have liked the wagon ride, since the training and trading of horses was such an important part of his life. Joe gave strict instructions that they had to keep Buck's head to the front of the wagon so as to lower the coffin into the grave with Buck's head at the end where the head marker was set. He explained that they would drive right up to the grave with the horses facing the head marker and stop with the wagon bed along side the open grave. All they had to do was remove the side board from the wagon, slide the coffin sideways, and lower it to the ground. The funeral home crew would take over from that point.

When Joe was satisfied that they had his instructions planted in our heads, he had them take the seats he had set aside. Everyone listened to the preacher tell what a fine fellow Buck had been and read from the Scriptures. Then, after all the people had passed by for a last look at Buck, Joe quietly closed the casket and motioned the pall bearers to pick it up.

At this point, Charlie took a long drink and said he couldn't help thinking that Buck looked a little strange lying there without a cigar in his mouth. None of the pallbearers could remember seeing Buck with a neck tie on or without a cigar between his teeth. Charlie ordered a round of drinks and returned to his story.

"Things went pretty well till we got to the end of the gravel road where the team and wagon were waiting. George and Clarence were at the head, and George slipped while trying to push the coffin into the wagon. If it hadn't been for one of Joe's workers' grasping George's side of the coffin, we would have dropped Old Buck right there. George fell flat in the mud, and somebody suggested that, perhaps, he had a couple of drinks to drive out the chill of the falling rain. George swore that he hadn't touched anything stronger than coffee since the day before. After cleaning some of the mud off of George, we trudged behind the wagon for what seemed to be a mile, but Joe said it was only a quarter. By the time we got to the grave yard, my shoes felt like they had picked up ten pounds of mud. Then, the wagon mired down about thirty or forty feet from Buck's opened grave. After walking around the wagon a couple of times, the teamster tried having the horses back up a step and then lunge into their collars in an attempt to jerk the wagon free of the soft mud. Finally, he said there was nothing to do but carry Buck the rest of the way, which we did with only one near disaster. As we had the coffin just about clear of the wagon bed, something caused the team to lunge again, and this time, without the weight of the coffin, the wagon seemed to spring forward, and we almost dropped Buck again. After some scrambling to regain our footing, which seemed to cause Buck's weight to shift a little to one end of the coffin, we managed to deposit our friend in his final resting place." After a deep sigh, Charlie continued.

"The preacher, who had followed along behind the wagon, read a few words from between the rain drops which had splattered onto his opened Bible from the edge of the tarp hastily stretched over the grave by the funeral home crew. As soon as the Bible was closed, we left for town, leaving the final burial to Joe's people. Nobody said much, except to remark on the last time they had seen Buck alive and what he had said to them. When we were all lined up at Jim Mac's bar for a toddy to warm our wet and aching bones, someone pointed our that George hadn't said a single word since we left Buck's grave.

George took a sip from his glass, shook his head like he was still trying to clear the rain out of his eyes, and stated, "I think we made a bad mistake out there at the grave yard. We headed Old Buck in the wrong direction."

"What do you mean?" asked several at the same time. We reminded George that we had done exactly like Joe had instructed us to do. Clarence even repeated Joe's final order to slide the coffin off of the side of the wagon so Buck's head would be at the head of the grave.

"That ain't the problem," said George. "We followed Joe's orders to a T, but we didn't follow the order Buck always gave us when he would leave us alone on a construction site. Don't you guys remember?"

"Sure!" said Clarence, "I've heard him say it a thousand times: 'Listen, boys! I can't be every where at once. In this kind of work something can go wrong and people can get hurt; so you've got to keep your eyes opened and think for yourselves.'"

From behind the bar, Jeff asked what all this had to do with heading Buck in the wrong direction. Jeff reasoned that, since Buck was in no condition to direct his own funeral, the pallbearers had to follow the man in charge, Joe VanNatta.

"That's just it!" George said in a loud voice. "We followed orders, but we didn't keep our eyes on the situation and think for ourselves when circumstances changed."

"So what was there to think about?" asked Troy, a long-time friend of Buck who had been listening. "Jeff, give George a drink to settle his nerves," drawled Troy. "We wouldn't want him to blow a gasket, or something."

George accepted the drink, but he would not give up his conviction that Buck had been buried with his feet toward the head of the grave. Finally, Jim Mac called for silence and ordered Jeff to pour a round for everyone at the bar, on condition that they would hear George out.

When the beer was foaming and the ice sparkling in the mixed drinks, George explained that Joe's instructions were perfect, except for one thing. The process for transporting the coffin from the hearse to the grave was shortened by one step after Joe issued these instructions, which caused a mismatch between process and instructions. As Joe had planned the operation in his mind at the funeral home, the wagon would make a 180 degree turn as it approached the grave so that the front of it (where the head of the coffin rested) would be pointed toward the head of the grave. But it never happened that way. The wagon mired down before it could be turned around; the coffin was lifted off the side of the wagon (just as Joe had said to do): so Buck was planted in the wrong direction.

After reviewing the sequence of actions involved in transporting Buck from the hearse to the grave several times, everyone agreed that George was right about Buck being planted in the wrong direction. Then, since they couldn't think of any way to rectify the situation without causing a lot of embarrassment and, perhaps, even reopening the grave to place the coffin in proper position, the friends of the deceased gathered at Jim Mac's bar that rainy afternoon began reciting situations in which Buck had demonstrated his ability to think for himself. Troy Killman said that his father, known affectionately as Uncle Billy, enjoyed telling how Buck had tried to convince a Baptist preacher that Heaven begins just a few feet above the Earth. Buck had based his argument on a quotation from the Bible to the effect that the fowls of the earth shall fly in Heaven. According to Uncle Billy, the minister was not convinced, and Buck was not really welcome at the local Baptist church until the appointment of a new minister. Clarence Bennett recalled how Buck had under bid all competitors on a project to demolish a tower at Southern Illinois University. However, the University awarded the contract to another bidder when they discovered that Buck's method of dismantling the tower would be to explode dynamite charges under one side of the base, which would drop the tower into an opened field between two classroom buildings. Buck explained that the process would be just like felling a tree just where you wanted it with the proper placing of wedges, but the SIU officials were not so confident. Troy told how Uncle Billy had watched Buck construct a well-digging machine when he was a young man and how he had earned his livelihood by digging wells for local farmers until he branched out into other types of construction.

The pallbearers and other friends continued to swap interesting stories of how Buck exercised his independence of thought and action. This story telling went on far into the night, with Jeff setting up another round at the expense of one or another of the patrons gathered at Jim Mac's Tavern. At last, somebody noted that George had not been participating in the conversation and asked if he were still worried about planting Old Buck in the wrong direction. "At first, I really felt bad-like we had let Buck down by turning him the wrong way in his grave--but, the longer I listen to you boys talk about the way Buck looked at life, the more certain I become that we done exactly as Buck would have told us to do it if he could have talked," said George, as his face relaxed into a smile. "You see," George continued, "Old Buck looked at everything from a different direction, anyhow; so I figure he's much more content looking up at the heavens in the opposite direction from all the other folks buried in that grave yard."

Alvin Roberts

THE HUNGRY HERD

Jerry kicked the snow from his boots just inside PK'S front door and announced, "It's colder than a well digger's ass out there." As he settled himself on a stool, Stan, the bar tender asked if he wanted a beer. Jerry said it was too cold for beer and ordered hot coffee, repeating, "It's colder than a well digger's ass out there."

"Don't you mean to say that it's colder than a witch's tit?" asked Stan as he deposited a steaming cup of coffee in front of Jerry. Jerry said he had heard that phrase about the well digger ever since he could remember. Stan replied that his grandpa topped that by always describing unusually cold weather as, "colder than a witch's tit."

This banter between Stan and Jerry stimulated a recitation of colorful phrases which those seated up and down the bar had learned from their elders. Some phrases common to most of the patrons were: "tight as the bark on a tree; too dumb to come in out of the rain; clear as mud; queer as a two-dollar bill;" and, "dumb as a box of rocks." Debbie said her uncle usually criticized ideas he thought were doomed to failure by saying, "That has about as much chance as a fart in a whirl wind." Tapping my empty mug on the bar to attract attention, I put forth two descriptive statements from my dad. To dramatically describe a miser, he would say "That man wouldn't pay a nickel to see Jesus Christ ride a bicycle!" When he wanted to tell someone that he absolutely would not loan money or provide any other help, Dad would look the person straight in the eye and state, "I wouldn't give you a bale of hay if you was a horse on a concrete pasture!"

This last statement shifted the conversation to examples of malnourished animals due to natural circumstances or the negligence of their keepers. Someone told a joke about a miserly old farmer who bought a team of mules because he heard they could live and work on very little feed. Wanting to condition his mules to exist on as little feed as possible, this farmer began reducing their feed by a few ounces each week. After several months, the feed store proprietor noticed that the farmer was buying no mule feed at all and asked if the farmer were buying his feed from another store. The farmer complained that, as soon as the mules learned to live without feed, they up and died.

This tale brought out robust laughter and much thumping on the bar for drink refills. A stranger, who said he had lived most of his life in North Dakota, told of a cold hearted rancher near Medora, North Dakota who was known to allow an entire heard of cattle to starve for lack of grain during long, sub-zero winters. He calculated that it was cheaper to buy a new heard than to pay for feed to be dropped from air planes. This evoked several graphic descriptions of how certain procedures should have been performed on various parts of the rancher's anatomy in order to teach him to be kind to animals.

All this talk about starving animals caused me to embellish an incident related by Gayle Johnson of Cobden, Illinois. Cobden is a picturesque little hamlet nestled in a valley surrounded by hills created by glacial deposits. There are many such valleys where lush grass is fed by meandering creeks which are filled by run-off from the surrounding hills. During the spring rains in March and April of 1937, the year of the Great Flood, some old timers swear that the grass grew a foot every week. 1993 seemed just as wet, although no one could confirm this one foot growth in a seven-day period. However, one seasoned resident remarked that the grass grew so fast that a heard of sheep grazing twenty-four hours a day would have been submerged by the growth before dry weather.

Into one of these secluded valleys rode a cattleman in a four-wheel drive Jeep trailed by a rented truck loaded with the family possessions. This truck had been driven from North Dakota by Rex Morgan, son of the Jeep driver. Rex had moved from Medora, North Dakota in 1990 to teach industrial arts at a local high school. He was so impressed with the grazing possibilities created by the annual rainfall of about forty-two inches that he persuaded his father, Frank, to purchase a farm and establish a small cattle business after his retirement from the English Department at Dickinson State Teachers' College in Dickinson North Dakota. Growing up on a small ranch near the Little Missouri River Bad Lands just east of the Montana-North Dakota border, Frank was astounded by the stark contrast between the bareness of his boyhood home, which received only twelve to fifteen inches of rain each year, and the moist, fertile valleys of Southern Illinois. Whereas it was necessary to possess hundreds of acres to provide adequate grazing for a hundred head of cattle in the arid land of the Little Missouri, Frank's first view of his son's new home convinced him that a hundred head of cattle could thrive here on less than a hundred acres. So, after his mother's death, it was not difficult for Rex to convince his father to retire from his teaching position and enter upon a venture which he had contemplated for many years.

Frank Morgan's life had been good. Two years in the military during the Korean War had enabled him to afford undergraduate and advanced degrees in English. After three years as an English instructor at the University of Arkansas, where he married Cathy O'Hara, he landed a teaching position at Dickinson, just thirty miles from his father's ranch, where his son Rex spent much of his free time learning about ranching and human values from his grand parents, just as Frank had done in the 1930's and 1940's. But the influence of his father had caused Frank's life to take a different path than he had planned during the long, pleasant days of riding fences, driving cattle from one pasture to another which had adequate grass, and performing other routine chores of ranching. Frank was at home on the range during high school and assumed that he would settle down to a rewarding existence, first as a partner with his father, and, at some time in the distant future, as the owner of the family spread. However, the Korean War interfered and his father began to persuade him to look for some occupation which was not so dependent on the weather, the Chicago live stock market, and other factors totally outside his control. Frank's mother, who had reveled in her role as a country school Marm, told of the joys of enabling children to expand their knowledge and understanding of the world around them as she sat in the family living room during the long winter evenings the year Frank came home from Korea. Her persuasion and the availability of the GI Bill motivated Frank to strike out for the University of Arkansas and a career as an English teacher. But he never totally forgot his adolescent desire to be a rancher, and he grasped at this original script as a way to restore some purpose and pleasure to his life after his wife's death.

So it was that Frank and Rex pulled up before the two-story farm house on an August afternoon in 1991 and began unloading Frank's furniture and other belongings under the expert direction of Rex's wife, Millie. "I still don't know what I'm going to do with all this furniture and this two-story monstrosity," Frank said for at least the twentieth time. Millie reassured him that he would be regularly visited by his grand children from their neighboring farm and entertaining his new neighbors, some of whom were professors at a near-by university.

"Listen, Pop", Rex joked, "there is a surprising number of eligible ladies in this neck of the woods. You may not be living by yourself for too long." Millie and Rex were right. Frank was seldom without a grandchild in the house, and he was soon involved in a writers' association where he and the other members took turns criticizing each others stories, poems and essays. He had taught courses in western writing, and his expertise in the techniques of such authors as Mark Twain, Zane Grey and Louis LaMour made him a vital resource in this writers' group. Also, he soon began to appear at social gatherings with an attractive, middle aged lady who taught poetry at a local junior college. They were married in the spring of 1992, and Frank soon learned that his two-story home was not any too large for the visiting children and grand children of his newly created extended family.

During the autumn of 1991, Frank spent his days making repairs to the barn and machine shed, strengthening his pasture fences and filling pot holes in the road leading into his farm. In the late spring of 1992, he began buying young Hereford cows as breeding stock to begin building his herd. By the spring of 1993, he had about twenty head heavy with calves and everything was going splendidly.

Buying the farm, breeding stock, and feed to sustain his cows during the winter, plus the cost of the honeymoon, and redecorating the house for the new bride had just about exhausted Frank's savings by the end of February, but he was sure the worst was over. The lush grass would sprout up with the spring rains, and the need for buying feed would be a thing of the past. Ethel would earn enough from her job at the junior college to tide them over until a few cows could be sold. Also, Frank planned to raise a few acres of corn and oats to relieve the need for buying feed for the coldest months of the next winter.

The spring of 1993 could not have began better for Frank's purpose, even if he could have written the weather reports himself. The rains began in early March and never let up. Within a week, Ethel and other members of the family began complaining about the constant inconvenience of the soggy roads, wet clothing, cancelled sports events and congealed sugar and salt. Frank, on the other hand, returned from inspecting the heard every morning whistling "Happy Days Are here Again." When he would hear the sound of rain on the porch roof as he and Ethel relaxed in the living room after dinner, Frank would usually remark, "Listen to that liquid money." Of course, Frank's optimism was due to the phenomenal growth taking place in the pasture and the constant munching of his cows on the abundant grass supply. One day, he told Ethel that, with all that fine nourishment, they were bound to have unusually big calves.

"I would settle for smaller calves and more sunshine," responded Ethel.

As the weeks passed, the cows continued to chew ravenously, and Frank continued to brag about the fine herd they were going to have for their first year of the ranching business.

55

But one morning, Ethel commented, "Not to rain on your parade, but the cows don't seem to be gaining any weight." While their stomachs seemed to be expanding, tactual examination revealed a softness of their stomachs rather than rapidly growing calves. In April, Frank observed that the cows actually seemed to be losing weight, and by mid May, he could count their ribs at fifty yards.

Things came to a head while Frank and Ethel were away for spring graduation at Dickinson State, where Frank was receiving an award. Although they had planned to stay an extra week to visit friends, a phone call from Rex the morning after graduation brought them back on the next available flight. Rex's voice was very tense on the phone. "Dad, there is something bad wrong with you herd. We might have to destroy them if they are infected with some kind of communicable disease." When Frank asked how bad things really were, Rex told him that five cows were already dead.

"Get a vet out there and contact the Agriculture Department at Southern Illinois University to find out what kind of tests we can run to determine the cause of this catastrophe!" Frank shouted into the telephone.

Rex was waiting with the jeep when Frank and Ethel landed in a rainstorm at the Marion-Herrin Airport three days later. Since the commuter plane only landed at Dickinson three times a week, Frank had not been able to connect with North West in the twin cities until the third evening after Rex's urgent call. He had spent most of the two intervening days at the college library reading about rare cow diseases. The rest of the time, he spent talking to local cattlemen about the same subject.

Before the Jeep was out of the parking lot, Frank was demanding a status report on the herd. "We have bad and possibly good news," Rex said, as he worked the Jeep into the traffic on Illinois Route 13. "The bad news is that we have lost two more cows. The bright side is that the tests so far have not identified any pathogens." This meant that, at least, there was no indication of a communicable condition. He went on to explain that Dr. Max Sanders, the vet who had gathered the blood samples, would be at the farm the following morning to decide the proper course of action.

Miracle of miracles, the next morning dawned without a cloud in the sky, and the heat of the sun had dried the grass by the time Doc Sanders pulled his van into the barn yard. "I'm surprised you were able to fly in that bad weather last night," he said to Frank as he climbed out of his Ford van and ambled toward the barn.

"Well, Doc, what's the verdict? Do the tests show anything new? Do you have any idea of what killed my cows?" Frank asked these questions without allowing Doc Sanders time to answer.

"I know exactly what killed your cows," Doc Sanders answered when Frank paused to breathe. "They died from one of the oldest conditions in the animal kingdom. When Frank asked if there were any treatment for those cows still alive, Doc drawled, "My prescription is a regular dose of corn and oats. You see, Mr. Morgan, your cattle are suffering from starvation."

Frank protested that he had observed these animals eating lush grass nonstop for months. "The trouble, Mr. Morgan, is that wet grass is all they have eaten, and that grass has grown so fast in this dark, rainy weather, it has almost no nourishment. Had them cows not been carrying calves, they probably would have survived, although they would have not been fat enough to market for a long time."

This story seemed to have stimulated the patrons' appetites because several ordered peanuts and popcorn with their next drinks. Gwynn, the bar owner, began setting free salsa and chips on the bar. "I better feed this hungry herd before they start chewing up the napkins," she laughed.

Alvin Roberts

DARE-DEVIL

"That's a damn good story," pronounced Mop Head, placing the manuscript on the bar.

"Don't lay those pages in the beer I spilled on the bar," I cautioned. We were having a drink at PK's Bar, and Mop had been chuckling about the realistic way I portrayed him in a short story in which he was able to extricate himself from under a fallen horse without incurring any serious injuries. He informed me that he could tell me several yarns which I could embellish with a little dialogue and scenery to make them as amusing as the one he had just read. I ordered another round and suggested he begin spinning a few of these yarns.

"We had a good number of unusual people in our little town," said Mop Head, "But there was one family that was more unusual than all the others. They were from Kentucky, and they were all unpredictable, free spirits. You never knew what they would do next. I'll tell you a couple of incidents to give a flavor of their different approach to life and end up with a real humdinger of a story."

Mop Head said that Carl, the old man, was reported to have been a bootlegger in Kentucky, but, somehow, he wound up as a policeman in Illinois. Carl couldn't read very well, and he had only completed the eighth grade, but he was a hard worker and very proud of his position on the police force. He took pride in enforcing the law to the letter, showing no favoritism to friend or foe. Because of his limited education and rural background, Carl often misunderstood situations, but his loyalty to upholding the law was unquestionable.

It was this tendency to misinterpret situations that resulted in a humorous incident which is still told down at the police station. The story goes that, one Tuesday afternoon, Carl was sitting in his police car in front of the Highway Cafe when a pretty young lady in a new 1965 Buick drove by just a little too fast. Feeling it was his duty to impress this inexperienced young adult with her responsibility for obeying the town speed limit, Carl pulled his police cruiser up behind the Buick and turned on both his spot light and siren. When she produced her driver's license, Carl studied it very thoroughly and then looked very sternly into her beautiful blue eyes.

"Not only are you going forty-five in a thirty-five mile zone, but you are not wearing your glasses, which your license plainly says is required for you to drive. I wonder if you even seen the speed limit sign without your glasses," Carl said.

"Oh, it's OK, officer," the girl explained. Looking straight at Carl with those baby blue eyes, she said confidentially, "You see, I have contacts."

Carl's reaction to this optometric information startled the young woman, causing her to draw herself back from the opened car window. He straightened up to his full six-feet, aimed his right fore finger at a point between the girl's beautifully proportioned breasts, and said in a loud, indignant voice, "Young lady! If you knew my record as an honest cop, you wouldn't dare to make a statement like that. I don't care who your contacts are! I'm giving you a ticket." Even after the startled speeder convinced Carl that she was referring to her corrective lenses by removing one for his inspection, he persisted in issuing a ticket. As he explained to the Chief, the girl should have seen the speed limit sign with her fancy, glasses tucked under her eye lids, so she was willfully exceeding the limit.

Carl's youngest son, Tobe (a name bestowed by his little sister who could not pronounce "Tobias") possessed his father's single-mindedness in accomplishing what ever he decided to do. He also had another strong character trait that often created conflict between him and Carl. Tobe had a vivid imagination which he consistently translated into bizarre and sometimes dangerous action. As was his custom, Carl often responded with extreme measures aimed at teaching his son to consider the consequences of acting out his fantasies. For example, one Saturday morning Carl was sleeping deeply after a twelve hour shift when he dreamed Tobe had fallen into a well and was calling for help.

It was Tobe calling, but not from the bottom of a well. Deciding to act out a mountain climbing scene from a movie, he had attached a rope and pulley to a post on the upstairs porch near Carl's bed room and was proceeding to lower himself hand-over-hand down the face of his make-believe mountain when his thumb got caught in the pulley. With his feet kicking wildly about six feet from the ground, Tobe was screaming "Help! My thumb: My thumb!"

Carl fought his way up through several levels of unconsciousness, leaped out of bed and bolted on to the upstairs porch. Immediately recognizing that Tobe had again got himself into a pickle of a mess by his crazy play acting, Carl picked up a hatchet and severed the rope, letting Carl fall in a heap into the yard. When Tobe showed signs of life by thrashing around on the ground and complaining that his thumb was probably broken, Carl said, "Remember how your thumb feels the next time you wake me up with your crazy play acting." He then marched back to bed and was snoring loudly in a few minutes.

Carl's admonition, reinforced by the need to wear a cast on his wrist for several weeks, seemed to have taught Tobe the wisdom of refraining from dangerous games. During the month of April, he was a model child, when compared with his former wild self. He went to school, completed his home work, and even helped his mother clear the table on one occasion. His most dangerous exploit during this period was jumping off of the back porch with an umbrella held over his head in order to experience the thrill of a parachute jump.

One afternoon, Tobe approached the school principal, Dan Abbot, on the play ground with the suggestion that a parachute event be added to the schedule of the up-coming field day competition on the last day of school. Explaining that he had already tried such a jump from the high back porch of his house, Tobe suggested that the contestants jump from the top step of the sliding board holding umbrellas to provide lift. Dan could use his stop watch to time the jumps. The boy who remained aloft longest would be the champ. Dan politely, but firmly, over ruled this idea as too dangerous, and nothing more was said about it. But Tobe continued to ponder various ideas for nontraditional events which would add spice and challenge to the Field Day Program.

One evening while browsing through a car racing magazine he found on the seat of Carl's police cruiser, Tobe read a notice of an up-coming television event in which Evel Knievel would drive off the end of a high platform and sail over twelve parked cars before making a four-point landing in the parking lot. How, wondered Tobe, could he persuade Mr. Abbot to add such an event to the Field Day Program (perhaps substituting bicycles for cars)? His conclusion was, that if Dan Abbot thought jumping off the sliding board was too dangerous, there was no way he would permit the riding of bicycles off the flat roof of the grade school. But, what about a surprise stunt in which a daring sixth grader sailed off the roof and landed safely in the grassy playground? Wouldn't this catch the attention of the sixth grade girls? So, Tobe turned his attention to devising a covert operation in which a surprise event of such magnitude would be remembered by not only the sixth grade girls, but by every girl in town, who would always admire the heroic daredevil who performed this dangerous feat.

To plan and carry out such a daring operation, Tobe would need to accomplish several objectives. First, there must be absolute secrecy, which meant he could not seek advice from a single other person. Second, he would have to have some time alone in the school building in order to find a way to get himself and his bicycle on to the roof unnoticed until he was ready to draw attention to himself performing the jump. To accomplish his first objective, Tobe began volunteering his services to help Harry Brown, the school janitor, bring his cleaning and other supplies up from the basement after school. This made it easy to wedge a small sliver of wood under a basement window so that it could be opened from the outside. One evening, he returned to the school, entered through the unlocked window, and searched until he located a small door leading on to the flat roof from a supply closet on the second floor. Luckily, the night before the final day of school was very dark with rain clouds. To get his bicycle up to the roof, Tobe again attached the pulley and rope used in his "mountain climbing" adventure. Attaching the pulley to the rain pipe at the top of the second floor, he was able to pass the rope around the pulley and attach one end to the frame of his bicycle. Standing on the ground by the bicycle, he proceeded to hoist it to the second floor. Attaching his end of the rope to a swing set located near the door leading into the first grade hall, he climbed back to the roof and hid the bicycle behind a chimney. He then disassembled his equipment and returned it to the family garage. As he drifted off to sleep, Tobe pondered how easy it would be to sneak up to the roof during the Field Day activities and perform his heroic deed. His last impression before sleep was of the hundreds of admiring faces gazing up at him as he sailed through the air to fame and glory.

Tobe was disappointed to hear rain still running off the house when he awoke to the smell of frying bacon and hurried through breakfast. A little rain was not going to interfere with his big chance to perform the most outstanding deed ever witnessed at the Eldorado Grade School Field Day. Taking several wire coat hangers from his closet and borrowing his mother's brightly colored umbrella from the hall closet, Tobe skipped to school, arriving even before the janitor, who showed up about 8:00 A.M. and admitted him through the basement. Pretending to go to his class room, Tobe ascended on up to the roof, where he attached the umbrella to the handle bars of his bicycle with the wire coat hangers to increase its gliding capacity. Noticing that the rain had stopped and feeling the heat of the sun on his back, Tobe knew this would be his finest day.

By ten A.M., the school yard was dotted with groups of students, parents and friends observing the various contests occurring in different areas. One of the most hilarious events was the greased flag pole climb. Most contestants would leap as high on the pole as possible, climb furiously until they lost momentum and began slipping slowly back down, picking up speed until they hit bottom with a thud. The boy who won was the tallest kid in the school, who leaped higher than any other contestant, and was wearing rough work gloves. The sack race, tug-of-war, and pole vault also attracted many spectators.

A number of students proudly wore blue, white or red ribbons by the time the spectators began to unpack picnic lunches as the noon school bell rang. Carl, who had volunteered to attend the festivities in case of civil or other disturbances, had parked his police car at the east side of the play ground and was asking Principal Dan Abbot if he had seen Tobe competing in the various events. If there was competition going on, Tobe was usually right in the middle of it. Dan said, come to think of it, he had not seen Tobe since school let out yesterday afternoon. About that time, Dan's youngest daughter, Lorie, who was in the third grade, tugged at her father's sleeve and asked, "Daddy, what's Tobe riding his bicycle around the school house roof for?"

His glance following Lorie's pointing finger, Carl roared "Tobe! Get the hell off that roof right now!" Responding to Carl's commanding voice and pointing fist, the crowd became riveted to the vision of Tobe circling the chimney on his bicycle with a brightly colored umbrella billowing above him. As he made his final turn around the chimney, Tobe accelerated rapidly and headed straight for the edge of the roof. Looking directly into the eyes of his spectators, Tobe emitted a long, triumphant shout: EEE-VELL K-NEE-VEL-L-L! ! !" And he sailed off of the roof. Instead of soaring far out over the play ground, Tobe and his flying bicycle seemed to hang upright for a fraction of a second and then drop straight down into a mud hole beside the roof rain spout. Even when it hit the ground with an explosive sound caused by the tires blowing, the bicycle and Tobe remained up right. Carl, who was the first to reach the accident site, soon discovered the reason for this upright landing. The bicycle wheels and both of Tobe's feet were firmly buried in the soft earth. When he was extricated from his earthly mooring, Tobe could not seem to stand alone; so, they carried him to the police car and took him to the hospital, where it was determined that he had broken both ankles.

Tobe's hospital was flooded with congratulatory letters from his school mates, most of them stating that Tobe's parachute leap had made this Field Day the most exciting of their school experiences. Before the summer was over and while Tobe was still walking on crutches, he made a written proposal to Principal Abbot to include the parachute jump as a regular Field Day event, with the contestants landing in an above ground pool in order to soften the impact and reduce injuries.

Alvin Roberts

ORCHIDS FOR VICKI

I met Vicki about four years prior to the hot summer afternoon when she told me a hilarious story about a trip she and her former husband took to Chicago. She first entered my awareness as the woman who came into the American Legion one Saturday afternoon in 1994 with several piano books tucked under her arm and proceeded to organize a sing-a-long. This was a welcome diversion from the usual diet of football blaring out of the two television sets located at opposite ends of the bar. She later confided that her excellent repertoire was the result of nine years of piano lessons and diligent practice which she did to avoid household chores regularly assigned to her siblings by her mother. During subsequent years, I learned to know and appreciate Vicki for characteristics other than piano playing. She is an amusing person who sees the humorous side of all questions regardless of their magnitude or solemnity. Vicki also derives pleasure from the use of humor and practical jokes to illustrate her ideas or reinforce her point of view. It is this little streak of devilment in her personality that created the event on which this story is based.

To truly savor the nuances and humor of this event, it is also necessary to have some knowledge of Carl, the other primary character. This understanding of Carl can help the reader to fully enjoy the interaction between him and Vicki. Born in Germany during World War II, he found little opportunity to apply his considerable intellectual talent either in the achievement of economic success or acquiring a university education in the devastation of post-war Germany. Carl knew he possessed the physical and mental traits to succeed. After all, his fore-bearers were successful scientists and military officers, and, even in the German defeats in both World Wars, his relatives had demonstrated brilliant military leadership against insurmountable odds. Carl knew he, too, could rise to the top if he could only get to America where opportunities were boundless for a young man with his talents and strength of character. His opportunity came when his father, a nuclear physicist, secured employment at a nuclear project in Tennessee.

Carl was 19 years old when he arrived in the United States. Finding that his German education was, in many ways, superior to that of his young American acquaintances, Carl began improving his English and was soon admitted to the School of Pharmacy at the University of Tennessee, where he worked hard and made better grades than most of his peers. His demanding study schedule limited Carl's social life to week-end beer parties and occasional dining at a German restaurant where he could enjoy the food of his home land, which Carl knew was much superior to American cuisine. After graduation, Carl worked for a time in a Nashville pharmacy, saving most of his earnings. When he learned from a former class mate at an alumni reunion that this friend's uncle was looking for a young pharmacist to take over his drug store located in a small southern Illinois town, Carl used his savings to buy a part interest in the store and moved to Vienna, Illinois, which pleased him because it, at least, was named after a prominent European city.

In general, Carl found life in rural America pleasing and rewarding. His energy and ingenuity substantially increased the pharmacy income over that received by his predecessor. He found his neighbors to be very similar in attitude, speech and demeanor to his associates back in Tennessee. Probably because of his economic success, self confidence, tall distinguished appearance, and excellent education, Carl was welcomed into the social and economic life of the community. Within two years of his arrival, he was a member of the Chamber of Commerce, treasurer of the Rotary Club, and had won election to the school board.

It was Carl's position on the school board which focused his attention on an attractive, bright-eyed young English teacher. He first noticed her when attending a high school play which she directed. He was taken with her mischievous sense of humor and willingness to defend her opinions. The girls back home in

Germany were more submissive and easier to dominate, but he soon found this spontaneous little English teacher to be much more stimulating and mysterious than those predictable Fraulein. Of course, the desirable creature was the heroine of our story, Vicki.

Shortly after his introduction to her at the school play, Carl glanced across the counter after pouring a milk shake for a varsity foot ball player, and there, perched on a stool, was the provocative English teacher. After soliciting Carl's opinion on the quality of the play he had attended at the high school, Vicki asked if he would agree to an interview for her column in the weekly paper which profiled local businesses and interesting persons in the community. Since Carl had migrated to America as a young man and had been able to acquire a professional education and achieve success as a local business man, she believed his story would be of interest to her readers and inspirational to her senior class whose members would be leaving for college or entering the workforce following the up-coming graduation. This interview was conducted in the relaxed atmosphere of the Four Seasons, a restaurant which advertised gourmet candle-light dining. The interview extended far into the evening and included after dinner cocktails.

Following several dinner dates, picnics, and excursions to Paducah, Kentucky and St. Louis, an announcement of the wedding of Carl and Vicki appeared in the local paper, and the couple moved into Carl's new house following the wedding, where their marital bliss was interrupted only occasionally by Vicki's obstinate refusal to agree that most things German were superior to their counterparts in the United States. Most of the time, however, Vicki kept her opinions to herself, although this repression tended to build a twinge of resentment and desire for reprisal. One evening after finishing a dinner composed of several German dishes personally prepared by Vicki, Carl announced they would be taking a trip to a school board convention in Chicago, "where they could enjoy some real German cuisine." This implication that her German dishes were inferior irritated Vicki, but she disguised her feelings, waiting for the right opportunity to even the score. Besides, wining and dining at the Palmer House, where the school board conventions were held, partly compensated Vicki for Carl's slight.

On the appointed day, Vicki and Carl arrived at the Amtrack Station in Carbondale about 4:00 O'clock A. M., parked in the long-term lot south of the station, and boarded the City of New Orleans. Breakfasting on eggs benedict, Carl looked leisurely out of the dining car window at the passing farms and announced that he would be dinning on quality German food this evening. Vicki reminded him that her light-weight evening gown was not suitable for traveling long distances in the Windy City. After a few sharp words were exchanged, Carl agreed to a compromise. They would dine at Trader Vick's in the Palmer House, where Vicki could show off her new outfit, this evening. Tomorrow, however, would be another matter. They would travel as far as necessary to enjoy the food and atmosphere of a quality German establishment. Vicki agreed, adding the provision that she would go to Marshall Field's while Carl was attending tomorrow's convention session and buy a warmer outfit more appropriate for German dining.

After checking into the Palmer House, Carl attended a caucus of Southern Illinois school board members, and Vicki visited several shops on the hotel concourse, buying gifts for friends, after which she returned to her room to dress for dinner. When Carl let himself into their room, he was pleasantly surprised to view Vicki posing before a floor length mirror in a red, satin dress and red velvet slippers with four-inch heels. They drank a toast with gin and tonic from the automated room bar, and proceeded to Trader Vick's located on the lobby floor. Seated at a secluded table, they perused the beverage menu, finally selecting a scorpion. When the waiter explained that this selection consisted of a variety of liquors in a bowl with four straws for communal consumption, Carl assured him they had spent a long, hard day and would have no difficulty consuming a beverage meant for four people. Vicki was ecstatic over the accessory, a beautiful orchid, which the waiter explained was presented by the management to those who ordered scorpions, as she deftly pinned it to the right side of her low-cut red dress. After further review of the menu and liberal consumption of the scorpion, Carl decided on London Broil, which he had heard was a favorite of King George who was, after all descended from German royalty. Vicki chose chicken Kiev and suggested they order another scorpion because she needed an orchid for the left side of her dress in order to provide symmetry. With a flurry, Carl waved over the waiter and ordered a second drink, reminding him of management's commitment to present an orchid with each scorpion. Just as Vicki had her second orchid strategically centered over her left breast, the salad arrived, and they busied themselves by satisfying a fierce hunger which had been building since their breakfast in the dining car about twelve hours before. The main course also was dispatched with alacrity, after which they resumed concentration on the remains of their second scorpion and ordered a third, which prompted the waiter to inquire solicitously if they had far to travel after dinner. When Carl assured him they were guests in the hotel, he quickly delivered a third scorpion with its orchid, which Vicki pinned below and between the other two, forming a v for "Vicki". Carl thought this was hilarious and told Vicki she was very clever.

Giddy from their drinks, they paid their check and giggled all the way to their room, where they planned to freshen up before going dancing. Carl poured himself a double scotch and pulled off his shoes to rest his feet while Vicki spent time in the bath room touching up her make up. This took longer than she expected because she had to remove a small stain from her dress and rearrange her orchids. At last, she made a grand re-entrance and discovered Carl had undressed and was snoring contentedly on the bed. This infuriated Vicki, who was wide awake and planning to make quite an impression on those stuffy school board members and their wives who would be attending the convention sponsored soiree in the Grand Ball Room. She knew any attempt to revive Carl was futile, but she had to do

71

something to reduce her frustration and express her displeasure to Carl. After finishing his double scotch, she experienced a revelation in the form of a visual image of Carl waking up to find orchids growing out of his under shorts. Well, she couldn't make them grow but pinning them would be good enough. Detaching the orchids from her dress, Vicki pinned one to each side of his shorts and one just below his belly button. After another scotch, and a period of uncontrollable laughing at the image of Carl stretched out on the bed with those orchids decorating his torso, Vicki slipped into bed and succumbed to exhaustion.

The only dream Vicki recalled when she awoke the next morning was of eating breakfast in the dining car of the City of New Orleans with Carl, who seemed to be unaware that he was wearing only his shorts with three orchids pinned to them. This dream reminded her of her impulsive retaliation against Carl for being a "party pooper." Sitting up carefully to minimize the throbbing in her head, she eased back the sheet to see if Carl was still wearing his corsage, and was startled to notice small specks of dried blood, Carl's blood, dotting the sheets. He had repeatedly pierced his skin with the orchid pins by rolling over in his sleep. Realizing that her joke had gone too far, Vicki agilely removed the pins and tossed the orchids into the waste can. She then snuggled back into bed, feigning sleep in the hope that Carl would not associate any of his discomfort with her when he awoke. When he drifted back into consciousness, his first impression was of Vicki sleeping peacefully beside him. All of a sudden, Vicki heard the bed-side lamp snap on and felt the covers being thrown back. She sat upright in bed when Carl shouted, "Vicki! Get out of that filthy bed immediately. We are checking out of this damn flea bag of a hotel today." When she reminded him that the convention would not be over until the next day, he replied. " I don't care! The last woman who slept here was having her menstrual period, and these shiftless maids did not have the decency to wash the sheets. This would never happen in a first-class German hotel."

In order to get Carl out of the room before he could make a scene with the maid (and possibly discover the real source of the blood specks on the sheets), Vicki told Carl she had a terrible headache and needed breakfast. Returning to their room after a leisurely breakfast, Carl found everything spotless, including the bed sheets, which he insisted on inspecting. The remainder of the convention was enjoyable. Vicki visited a museum and did some more shopping. They had dinner at Berghoff's that evening and returned home on the train the next evening. Vicki waited several years to tell Carl the whole story about the spots on the hotel bed sheets, carefully choosing a time when he was in a particularly good mood.

Alvin Roberts

THE BOATMAN'S LADY

It is hard to say who is the main character in this yarn: John Truman McGee, a colorful river-boat man, who boasted that he could out swear, out fight, out work and out screw any boatman on the Mississippi; Dorothy Farmer, a retired nurse for whom John Truman had an insatiable physical attraction, even though she was almost twice his age; Jerry, Dorothy's son, who gave up a good bar tending job at a popular night club to try his hand as a black jack dealer in Hot Springs, Arkansas; or Vicki, the popular piano player who gave up the spotlight and applause to marry Jerry and settle into the house wife routine. Maybe the reader will decide it was none of the above and choose Dorothy's toy poodle, Foofoo, as the real tragic heroine.

Where to begin? As John Truman would say, "Keep it simple, stupid! Begin at the beginning!" So, we will start with Dorothy, the oldest character in this little band of pleasure seekers. Dorothy was the eldest daughter of Gladys and John Farmer, a Hell-fire preaching Baptist minister in Hazzard County, Kentucky. Because her father thought women had no business working outside the home and didn't believe in medicine, preferring to leave healing to the Lord, Dorothy ran away from home to study her chosen vocation of nursing. After graduating from a nursing school in Paducah, she settled in Mound City, Illinois, where she became a public health nurse. Her son, Jerry, was the result of an affair with a local doctor when she was forty-two and thought her child-bearing days were over. He refused to leave his wife when he learned that Dorothy was pregnant, which so angered Dorothy that she decided to bestow her maiden name of Farmer on her son. She sent a baby picture and a copy of the birth certificate to her father, "just to irritate the hypocritical old bastard," she laughingly told her friends.

As the years passed, Dorothy's increasing income enabled Jerry to enjoy most of the possessions and social activities, such as dances, cars, girls and booze, which were available to the more affluent teenage population. He was a good student, especially in math and science, but he announced during his senior year in high school that he had an offer as a used car salesman after graduation. This job lasted for about ten years before he took a job as bartender at the Paradise Club, where he had been spending a good part of his spare time playing black jack and poker, which consistently netted him a recreational income.

Jerry eased into a routine of work and pleasure during the next couple of years, continuing to reside with Dorothy, who had retired and enjoyed fixing breakfast for Jerry, who awoke about 10:00 A.M., read the paper, discussed the former night's events at the Paradise Club, and then went to work at 3:00 P.M. He worked until eleven and then alternated between playing black jack and romancing one of the waitresses or female customers. Jerry continued to maintain this satisfying life of work, pleasure and security until two events brought about drastic changes in his lifestyle.

The first, and most stressful, event was the arrival of John Truman McGee during a Civil War celebration. Since retirement, Dorothy had become involved with a group which reenacted Civil War scenes at an abandoned warehouse which was used as a Union Hospital during "The War between the States". She and her group dressed in period costumes and recreated the medical care delivery system for the union soldiers. They also participated in ceremonies at the National Cemetery located at the junction of routes 37 and 51 between Mound City and Mounds. John Truman had been dispatched to Mound City to assist in moving some barges from the small ship yard at Mound City to Memphis, Tennessee. After a few drinks in a local bar, he followed the crowd to the Civil War celebration, where he first saw Dorothy and went absolutely "ga ga". When the ceremonies were concluded, he marched straight up to Dorothy and announced in a loud voice, "I'm John Truman McGee from Tennessee, and I'm goin' to marry you because you're the purdiest woman I've ever seen in my life!" Dorothy proceeded to slap his face, which elicited a hearty laugh from John Truman and a promise to be at her house at six that evening to take her to dinner at Harper's Cafe in Cairo, which he did. Dorothy never explained why she softened her attitude toward John Truman between the scene at the war ceremony in the afternoon and his arrival at her door promptly at six that evening. It may have been the toy poodle, Foofoo, which he presented to her as "an engagement present". She eventually became so attached to this little creature that she was almost never seen without her.

After that first date, John Truman was at Dorothy's house when he was not working as a deck hand on a tug boat. He was in town ten days out of thirty, and, during those ten days, life for Dorothy and John Truman was one continuous party. They ate frog legs at Harper's, danced at The Purple Crackle and held house parties for their friends. When John was on river boat duty, he sent printed letters to Dorothy every day and insisted that she print daily love letters to him. He insisted on print correspondence because he said that he could not read script, which he called, "writin'", and said that it looked like a tangled roll of fishing line. It wasn't that John Truman was actually illiterate; he borrowed western books from the library, which he called "readin' matter." As John explained, I can read readin', but I kaint read writin'."

In the beginning, Jerry really enjoyed the fast life carried on by Dorothy and John Truman, but the fast pace, coupled with his routine at the club, began to exhaust him. He had been dating the most recent piano player at the Paradise Club, a pretty, diminutive, bright-eyed girl named Vicki, who had her own apartment. Both were impulsive, and Jerry was tired of living with his mother, so one Saturday night they eloped. They were married in Paducah, Kentucky, and, the following Wednesday, they moved into Vicki's apartment. Jerry continued to increase his winnings at the black jack table, and his employer finally asked if he would like to try his hand as a dealer at a club in Hot

Springs, Arkansas, which was the second life-changing event for Jerry. Although there was no immediate employment for Vicki at the new club, they made the move and were able to survive.

While Vicki and Jerry were acclimating themselves to their new community, the relationship between John Truman and Dorothy began to deteriorate, primarily because of John's growing jealousy. Perhaps he had too much time to speculate on Dorothy's activities during his tours of duty aboard the tug boat. He began to accuse her of dating other more educated, polished men during his absence. Dorothy finally agreed to close her house and move to an apartment which John rented in Memphis, the home port of the tug boat company which employed him. She told Vicki in a letter that she hoped John Truman would not be so jealous with her living closer to his work. It was not long, though, before her letters reported he was accusing her of meeting men at the Peabody Hotel and other popular gathering places around Memphis. One night, Jerry received a frantic phone call at his club; Dorothy insisted that John was threatening to shoot her if he saw her even talking to the man he accused her of flirting with. She hysterically begged Jerry to rescue her and take her back to her home in Mound City. After reviewing the content and tone of this call with Vicki, they packed and headed to Memphis in Vicki's old Ford.

They almost succeeded in their rescue, loading Dorothy and Foofoo in the back seat and as many possessions as they could into the trunk of the old Ford. The car chase was caused by the note Dorothy left under John Truman's pillow. She did not tell them about this note until they spotted John Truman's ancient red Buick convertible overtaking them at a speed of at least ninety miles per hour. There was no chance of out running John because the Ford needed a valve job, and its top speed was about sixty. Jerry decided to just keep going, hoping that John Truman, who was now passing them at high speed and then slowing to force them to stop, would be picked up by a cruising state policeman.

The tragedy occurred when John passed them on the right shoulder because a truck was passing in the left lane. Vicki, riding in the front right passenger seat, rolled down her window and shouted, "Look out, you crazy son-of-a-bitch!" At that instant, the toy poodle decided to leap from Dorothy's shoulder, where she was perched, to the front seat and was whisked out the car window. Dorothy screamed as the fluffy little body sailed over the convertible and disappeared into the tall grass. Both John Truman, who was startled as the dog flashed past his nose, and Jerry quickly swerved into a truck stop just beyond the point where the dog flew out the window.

At first, assuming that her favorite companion (besides John Truman) had been killed by the accident, Dorothy insisted that a thorough search of the entire area be conducted. Because of her distraught condition, even the truck drivers joined in the search, but no trace of Foofoo was ever discovered. Dorothy reasoned that, having vanished into thin air, Foofoo had been saved by divine providence, and, thereafter, insisted that her spirit attached itself to the dog's collar, which was whisked off by the wind as the animal was blown from the car. She wears this collar around her right arm and says that she feels that Foofoo is always with her.

Her other favorite companion, John Truman also remains with her. He was so remorseful over the grief he inflicted on Dorothy that he quit his job as a deck hand so that he could always be available to meet Dorothy's every desire. In fact, John Truman was so contrite that he was never again heard accusing Dorothy of dating other men, but such accusations were not necessary because she was rarely out of his sight.

Alvin Roberts

ABOUT THE AUTHOR

Born in 1930 in the depth of "The Great Depression", Alvin Roberts came in this world face to face with the dual challenges of poverty and blindness. Growing up in an era when story telling and performing country music were major pastimes in the succession of taverns and lunchrooms operated by his parents, he quickly learned to play the guitar and remember yarns. When blindness necessitated the learning of typewriting in order to prepare homework assignments, Alvin logically began using the stories from adults for practicing typing. His first publishing success was a "tall tale", submitted at the suggestion of his sixth-grade teacher, which won second place in a liar's contest.

With assistance from the Illinois Division of Rehabilitation and earnings from performing country music in local night clubs, Mr. Roberts completed a Master's Degree in Education from Southern Illinois University at Carbondale. He has completed forty-six years of civil service, working in a succession of six different Illinois governmental departments. Prior professional publications include twenty-five articles in professional journals of rehabilitation and two books, <u>Psycho-social Rehabilitation of the Blind</u> (Charles C. Thomas, 1973) and <u>Coping With Blindness</u> (SIU Press, 1998).

Mr. Roberts is currently employed as a Quality Assurance Administrator of the Illinois Bureau of Blind services and resides in Carbondale, Illinois. His two daughters, Hope Silkwood and Lydia Hazel, together with their six children, reside in the Carbondale area as well.